I0151827

Love's True Meaning

The Message of *Humanae Vitae*
50 Years on

Fr Anthony Doe

All booklets are published
thanks to the generosity of the supporters
of the Catholic Truth Society

CTS

Contents

ISBN 978 1 78469 576 7

A Prophetic Vision

In his second letter to his beloved disciple Timothy, St Paul is very clear in his exhortation:

> Before God and before Christ Jesus who is to be judge of the living and the dead I put this duty to you, in the name of his Appearing and of his kingdom: proclaim the message and, welcome or unwelcome, insist on it.[1]

As we reflect upon the life of the Church over the centuries we see clearly that it is precisely the fidelity of those who are called to present the life of faith, even in the face of opposition, that affirms the Church's true identity, and enables it to grow in the truth of the Gospel, which is, of course, the life of Jesus Christ our Saviour. It is this life of the Risen Lord, the life that expresses the total self-giving love of the Father, that enables every individual to find the true meaning of their existence, which is rooted not in this world but in the Kingdom of God itself. It is the proclamation of this truth that has confronted the Church throughout the ages with all forms of rejection, from ridicule to outright violence – the same forces that Jesus himself had to contend with, and which finally ended in his death. As a result, as St Paul makes clear further on in his exhortation to Timothy:

> The time is sure to come when, far from being content with sound teaching, people will be avid for the latest novelty and collect themselves a whole series of teachers according to their own tastes… Be careful always to choose the right course; be brave with trials; make preaching the Good News your life's work, in thoroughgoing service.[2]

When Blessed Paul VI published his encyclical *Humanae Vitae* fifty years ago this year, he did so in the face of opposition and anger that were expressed not only by influential voices and organisations outside the Church but also within it. His presentation of the sacredness of marriage as the very centre of the movement of life-giving love and his clear condemnation of the use of all methods of contraception as damaging forces to the integrity of this love were seen as messages that no longer had any credible value in the face of the modern interpretations of sexuality and marriage in the contemporary world. Marital love and family life were increasingly understood within a context that was placing pragmatic social and economic values at the centre of human welfare.

By the end of the 1950s the age of post-war austerity, certainly in Western Europe, was slowly making way for growing affluence, with a real desire for material prosperity at all levels of society. Through the media and the world of entertainment, lifestyles that facilitated a new sense of freedom and personal pleasure were being presented as ideals to be aimed for. This was the beginning of the strong hedonistic element in Western culture that has continued to flourish, deeply affecting the ways of life and patterns of thinking of many people. It was into this context, in the early 1960s, that the contraceptive pill found a natural welcome and joined all the other forces that were re-shaping people's understanding, not only of marital love, but of all relationships where the desire for sexual intimacy was present.

As a consequence the exclusively physical dimension of sexuality, with all its emphasis on genital gratification, has now gradually accelerated to the point where many people are unable to embrace the deeper dimensions of the gift. High levels of promiscuity, the breakdown of marriage and family life, the increasing sexualisation of young people in schools and on university campuses and the lack of true reverence for life, which is expressed through abortion, are all symptoms of this tragic reality. Furthermore, it has become very clear within the Church that the development of lifestyles that sit comfortably now with these symptoms has damaged many people's openness to the life of faith and a genuine loving relationship with God. As a result, the lapsation rate of Catholics, certainly in the Western world, has greatly increased. Finally, all these factors were alluded to strongly in his encyclical where Blessed Paul VI gives us a strident warning of the grave consequences that would flow from the adoption of artificial birth control within married life. It is now vital, therefore, for us within the Church, to find the creative grace-filled response to this prophetic warning and so encourage our brothers and sisters to find the life-giving meaning of sexuality in all its depth. It is when this slowly comes alive that all the destructive forces, particularly contraception, that have robbed sexuality of its true meaning can then be recognised and confronted.

What Does Love Mean in a Secular Culture?

The opposition that the encyclical received, as has already been stated, did not just come from outside the Church but also came from within it. We must remember that it was written three years after the close of the Second Vatican Council, years that were full of turmoil but also years that had an air of excitement – something that was certainly encouraged by the secular culture of the mid to late sixties. The whole combination of the drive for increasing prosperity, new political movements and the growing influential power of the media was constantly emphasising the importance of exercising personal freedom, in relation not only to choice of lifestyles but also to adherence to personal belief systems. Liberation from constraints of whatever kind was seen as the ultimate value that could facilitate personal happiness and fulfilment. Sadly, this notion of freedom was based primarily on a purely superficial subjective experience of self-realisation, without the demands of external responsibility or commitment playing an important role. Any suggestion of relating the concept of freedom to objective norms or the constraints of disciplinary structures was increasingly frowned upon. Liberation from the old orders of the past, therefore, had an air of real excitement and expectancy that captivated the hearts and minds of people of all ages and backgrounds and definitely had a powerful influence on many in the Church. Unfortunately, the legacy of this movement still continues today.

What we can now see is that this understanding of liberation with all its dynamic expectancy joined forces with the immediate post-conciliar spirit that was still in its earliest phase of development. It encouraged an interpretation that was in compliance with "the spirit of the age" in which freedom of choice and the centrality of personal interpretation of objective truths were seen as essential features of the spirit of renewal. What is now clear is that the pre-conciliar Church, in many countries, was experienced as extremely controlling and often presented the life of faith in a harsh and legalistic manner, emphasising the centrality of the law and its maintenance at any cost. This frequently resulted in the exclusion of a life-giving presentation of God as the true source of liberation in his healing power and his fundamental desire to unite every human being with himself in a relationship of total merciful love. It powerfully affected the way many members of the Church interpreted the teaching on sexuality in all its aspects. Constantly presented within the constraints of the sixth and ninth commandments, sexuality ended up being seen by many people as an evil in itself, except within the strict bounds of marital fidelity. Hence feelings of guilt and shame leading to a constant fear of condemnation prevented a truly positive embrace of sexual instincts and drives that could be understood calmly, and creatively integrated within the objective moral teaching of the Church.

All these factors understandably nurtured a deep desire for change in the hearts of many Catholics who were yearning for a greater sense of personal freedom. What is now clear is that contraception was seen as a liberating component in the development of a new attitude to sexuality in which married couples could exercise a new form of responsibility in shaping their marital relationships and the production of families. All the other pragmatic forces referred to previously, particularly the social and economic, reinforced the practical legitimacy of contraceptive methods, offering a totally reasonable justification. However, what was of much greater significance, and which lay under the surface, was the severance of the pleasurable aspect of physical sexuality from a true sense of loving commitment to another person that facilitates its deepest expression in marital fidelity and the gift of creating new life. This gave the whole physical dimension of sexual pleasure an autonomy, freeing it to be experienced in its own right and as an end in itself. It was this separation that subtly reduced the dominance of shame and guilt that clearly made contraception an extremely attractive option for many people. It was seen as an intrinsic part of the renewal movements that were coming alive in the Church, enabling its members to live their lives of faith in communion with the modern world's understanding of fulfilment and happiness.

Opposition to the Meaning of
Humanae Vitae

During the years prior to the publication of the encyclical, therefore, both a desire and an expectancy that the Church would be willing to change its fundamental teaching, as outlined in Pope Pius XI's encyclical *Casti Connubii*, had increasingly gathered momentum. These sentiments had been present among members of the commission that Blessed Paul VI had assembled to reflect upon the contraceptive issue prior to his writing of the encyclical. Therefore, when it was published, proclaiming the traditional catholic teaching on sexuality and moral principles with a clear presentation regarding the spiritual integrity of marriage and the transmission of life, expressed in terms of the natural law of the Church, the negative reaction in many quarters was considerable. As has already been stated, the belief in a person's right to exercise personal freedom without automatic recourse to objective moral values, not only within the marriage but also outside the marital relationship, was becoming the norm for many people by the late sixties, particularly in the case of contraception. We can now see all too clearly the terrible damage, both socially and spiritually, this re-interpretation of freedom, particularly in a relational context, has wrought in the lives of people of all ages since that time. The breakdown of the traditional concept of marriage, leading to the fragmentation of family life with its severely destructive effects, emotional and psychological, in the lives of increasing numbers of children, has created a culture of instability that has increased the illusion that personal freedom must be exercised at all costs in order to compensate for the lack of a true sense of fulfilment.

The increasing addiction to the virtual world of the internet – in particular to pornography – that damages many people's capacity for genuine loving relationships is now one of the clearest examples of how this sense of freedom is exercised at the cost of healthy human development. As the therapeutic world knows only too well, direct human interaction is vital for personal growth in all its aspects. Without the gift of personal encounter with "the other" the real truth and mystery of the uniqueness of a person is unable to be touched and brought alive, and its inability to grow creates a deep interior sadness that is often not acknowledged but is nonetheless always present in a person's life. It is clear that at the time of the encyclical's publication these effects had yet to have the highly disruptive influence that we are now used to and that is taken for granted in our society. It has also now become clear that it was this lack of concrete experience that undoubtedly contributed to the reactive response of many who opposed the encyclical's message. However, now that we have witnessed all these negative developments over the past decades, in lifestyles that reveal all the tragic symptoms of instability, it is crucial that the prophetic truth of Blessed Paul VI's message should be not just re-assessed but fully embraced within a true spirit of love.

The Two Major Themes of Vatican II

In spite of the turmoil that erupted in the Church during the years immediately following the Second Vatican Council, there was never any doubt that the Holy Spirit was responsible for the Council's inauguration. It is the task of the Holy Spirit to arouse in all of us a deep desire to search for the truth of the Gospel message and a willingness to work with strength and patience to embrace it. It was after the Council had come to an end and the publication of its main documents had started to gain a wide circulation that its essential themes began to be recognised as creative sources for future development. What particularly stands out as a fundamental expression of the conciliar spirit are the opening words of *Lumen Gentium*, the Dogmatic Constitution on the Church:

> Christ is the light of humanity and it is, accordingly, the heart-felt desire of this sacred Council, being gathered together in the Holy Spirit, that by proclaiming his Gospel to every creature (cf. *Mk* 16:15) it may bring to all men the light of Christ which shines out visibly from the Church.[3]

It is fair to say that all the other major documents are in some way rooted in this truth and continually reflect it both

directly and indirectly, emphasising the true meaning of
the Council, which is the bringing alive in every dimension
of human experience of the living presence of Jesus Christ
for the world. This connects powerfully with the other
central truth that complements it, in personal terms, for
every member of the Church, namely the universal call to
holiness, which appears later in the same document:

> Therefore all in the Church, whether they belong to the
> hierarchy or are cared for by it, are called to holiness
> according to the apostle's saying: "For this is the will of
> God, your sanctification. " (*1 Th* 4:3 cf. *Ep* 1:4)[4]

And further on in the same document this second truth
is repeated:

> It is therefore quite clear that all Christians in any state
> or walk of life are called to the fullness of Christian life
> and the perfection of love, and by this holiness a more
> human manner of life is fostered also in earthly society.[5]

These two central themes are of particular significance
as we continue to reflect on the importance of *Humanae
Vitae*. The perfection of love, which is the essence of
holiness, can only come alive once Jesus Christ has been
able to establish the gift of his presence deep within a
person. When this takes place a light then shines out into
the world, a truth that echoes the words of Jesus to his
disciples in St Matthew's Gospel, "You are the light of
the world... Let your light so shine before men that they

may see your good works and give glory to your Father in heaven."[6] This only becomes possible when a person is able to receive the gift of Jesus's personal love growing within them, and this takes place as he slowly heals the wounds of sin and darkness, bringing a new sense of life and freedom into the very centre of their being. This is the truth that is stated so clearly in St John's Gospel when Jesus presents himself as the Good Shepherd: "I have come that they may have life, and have it to the full."[7] In his Apostolic Exhortation *Evangelii Nuntiandi*, written on the tenth anniversary of the Second Vatican Council, Blessed Paul VI says when referring to the Council:

> [T]he objectives [of the Council] are definitely summed up in the single one; to make the Church of the twentieth century even better fitted for proclaiming the Gospel to the people of the twentieth century. The Gospel being the Good News in which Christ proclaims salvation, the great gift of God which is liberation from sin and the Evil One, in the joy of knowing God and being known by him, of seeing him and being given over to him.[8]

In this statement it is clear that proclaiming this message is integral to the call to holiness of life which is none other than the proclamation of the living presence of Jesus Christ who, as we know, heals all the different aspects of human disorder, as a total expression of his love. Later on in his exhortation Blessed Paul VI states this even more clearly:

Finally, the person who has been evangelised goes on to evangelise others. Here lies the test of truth, the touchstone of evangelisation – it is unthinkable that a person should accept the Word and give himself to the Kingdom without becoming a person who bears witness to it and proclaims it in his turn.[9]

The Call to Holiness and Mission

The development of these fundamental themes has been a major enrichment of a deeper understanding of the gift of baptism, which is an immersion in the healing power of Jesus Christ. It is when this gift, in all its dimensions, begins to come alive that a new love for others begins to grow within the human heart, a love that moves a person to give of themselves, especially to those who are most in need. This love is nothing less than the presence of the Risen Lord who, having united the person to the healing power of his death on the cross, then shares the gift of love that comes from the resurrection. Pope St John Paul II, in *Redemptoris Missio*, points out that "All the Evangelists, when they describe the Risen Christ's meeting with his Apostles conclude with the missionary mandate, 'All authority in heaven and on earth has been given to me. Go therefore and make disciples of all the nations... And lo, I am with you always, to the close of the age' (*Mt* 28:18-20)."[10] He then points out that the mission of the apostles is the work of the Holy Spirit who, after the Ascension of Jesus into Heaven, manifests his power among the disciples at Pentecost, "to fill them with a serene courage that impels them to pass on the experience of Jesus and the hope which motivates them". On a final note Pope Francis in his encyclical *Evangelii Gaudium*, reflecting on the presence of goodness, has this to say:

> Goodness always tends to spread. Every authentic experience of truth and goodness seeks by its very nature to grow within us, and any person who has experienced a profound liberation becomes sensitive to the needs of others. As it expands, goodness takes root and develops. If we wish to lead a dignified and fulfilling life, we have to reach out to others and seek their good.[11]

This connection between the universal call to holiness and the universal call to mission is central to our understanding of the Church's renewal initiated by the Vatican Council. It was Fr Avery Dulles SJ, a Jesuit theologian who died in 2008, who once commented that the most significant change that has occurred in the Church since the Vatican Council is the shift from a static institutional model of being Church to an evangelistic self-understanding. It is an evangelism that is now recognised universally as "new": new in its ardour, new in its methods and new in its expression. As Pope St John Paul II clearly points out in *Redemptoris Missio*, "An essential characteristic of missionary spirituality is intimate communion with Christ."[12] It is this powerful emphasis on personal relationship with Christ as the starting point as opposed to on an adherence to dogmatic teaching, thereby rooting it in his salvific love for the world, that shapes the newness of evangelisation in different ways, giving it that "new" energy. It is the revelation of his salvific message that understands, with his wisdom, the world's need for healing and new life, and the ways in which evil creates lifestyles that prevent the spiritual goodness from coming alive in people, both in the Church and in the world. It is once this personal message of love and healing is communicated through individual witness of his presence, combined with a sensitive awareness of another person's suffering and need for new life, that the objective teaching of the Church's wisdom has a life-giving context in which the message can be creatively digested and come alive.

Jesus the Healer of the Wounds of Sin

The universal call to holiness is the invitation to share totally in the love that God has for each human being, who has been created in his image and likeness. This, as we know, slowly takes place as Jesus, who embodies the Father's love for us, begins to unite us with himself in a total union of love. This takes place in a profoundly intimate and personal way as he begins to free us from all the complex effects of Original Sin, which are deeply rooted within the fabric of our humanity. Now the image and likeness of God within us is expressed in our capacity to love and be loved unconditionally in such a way that the true mystery of our being and the Being of God himself is revealed in a joyful ecstatic union of spiritual love that will never end. It is also manifested in the human capacity to generate life physically when a man and a woman come together in a physical union of love that enables God to create a new life, once again in his own image and likeness. Jesus alone can fully bring alive in us these experiences of love, enabling us to celebrate our uniqueness and freedom in such a way that will give us the desire to bring these gifts alive in others.

The Book of Genesis makes it extremely clear that it is precisely in these areas of loving that Satan manifested his power to seduce and misrepresent the truth. Adam and Eve, our first parents, were lured into a world of denial and illusion. Misrepresenting God as someone to fear and reject, they were tempted and they tragically succumbed to a totally false understanding of love and freedom as experiences that did not flow from the intimate loving union with their Creator but had to be generated by self-will and the need to experience pleasure for its own sake. The human race, therefore, suffering the inheritance of this appalling seduction, continues to be vulnerable to the power of Satan with all its tragic consequences. However, it is vital for us to remember that the capacity to be drawn into the unconditional loving union with God still remains present in every one of us deep within the essence of our humanity, and it is Jesus who has the power to activate it and bring it into the fullness of life.

In the opening chapter of the Conciliar Document *Gaudium et Spes* the effect of sin is made very clear:

Man therefore is divided against himself. As a result the whole life of man, both individual and social, shows itself to be a struggle, and a dramatic one, between good and evil, between light and darkness. Man finds that he is unable of himself to overcome the assaults of evil successfully, so that everyone feels as though bound by chains. But the Lord himself came to free and strengthen man, renewing him inwardly and casting out the "prince of this world".[13]

This takes place as a new internal unity and sense of freedom that begins to come alive within the depths of a person, made possible by the unconditional love of Jesus touching the wounds of this division. As every human being knows only too well there is a fundamental conflict between the physical and spiritual, body and soul, which generates a restlessness and lack of inner tranquillity. The temptation is to find quick solutions to the discomfort that is present through compensating experiences that give immediate pleasure – exciting distractions that in the end only increase the lack of unity and inner peace. Jesus, through his own transfigured humanity, is the one who has the power to address this conflict by creating a new unity in a person: a power to love, which can bring body and spirit together in a totally new way.

What is Love?

Pope Benedict XVI in his encyclical *Deus Caritas Est* opens with a very important reflection on the two aspects of love, *eros* and *agape*: "*eros*, as a term to indicate 'worldly' love, and *agape*, referring to love grounded in and shaped by faith".[14] The former has often been described as "ascending love", its possessive and covetous aspects rooted in human desire for ecstasy and happiness at all costs, the latter as "descending love", described as totally self-giving and filled with desire to be there for "the other", seeking their happiness as the priority. In his reflection, carefully using ethical and biblical commentators, Pope Benedict demonstrates how the Fathers of the Church, within a spiritual context, did not see these two aspects as totally distinct to the point of being in opposition. On the contrary, using Jacob's ladder in the Book of Genesis as a potent symbol, they saw an "inseparable connection between ascending and descending love, between *eros* which seeks God and *agape* which passes on the gift received, symbolised in various ways".[15]

Pope Benedict then develops this theme of union, showing that the love God had for Israel was clearly erotic and moreover eclectic for, as he puts it, "God chooses

Israel and loves her – but he does so precisely with a view to healing the whole human race. God loves, and his love may certainly be called *eros*, yet it is also totally *agape*."[16] Within the context of this unitive reflection he then points out clearly that *eros*, as we all know, is rooted in man's nature, and it is *eros* that drives him to seek for a woman, then becoming one with the object of his desire. From the natural and total expression of *eros* the marriage bond is created in which *eros* finds its creative identity in the total commitment to the welfare of "the other". As Pope Benedict states clearly: "Marriage based on exclusive and definitive love becomes the icon of the relationship between God and his people and vice versa."[17]

This union presented in *Deus Caritas Est* highlights clearly the nature of unconditional love, in its most creative form. Pope Benedict then brings the first section of the encyclical to a close by placing the living presence of Jesus, as witnessed by us in his ministry in the Gospels, at the centre of this movement. He demonstrates how the Lord in his total self-gift embodies the fullness of the Father's love, the union of *eros* and *agape* in the most radical form in his death on the cross. It was there that the ultimate power of all the destructive forms of self-centredness, which tear apart and isolate the two essential aspects of love and which reside in every human being, was eliminated. It was then in his death that the ultimate power to destroy the essence of love, through Satan's exploitation, was eliminated. As Pope Benedict puts it, "By contemplating the pierced side of Christ (cf. *Jn* 19:37) we can understand the starting point of this encyclical: 'God is love' (*1 Jn* 4:8). It is there that this truth can be contemplated. It is from there that our definition of love must begin. In this contemplation the Christian discovers the path along which his life must move."[18] This is then nurtured through the living presence of Jesus in the Eucharist – the celebration of his death and resurrection, the source of nourishment for this gift of love to grow within ourselves. We are then able to love God and our neighbour with a love deep within us that brings alive our true personal identity that has been created to give life in all its forms. We will now reflect upon this more deeply.

The Gift of Sexuality

The power to love is rooted in the supreme gift of sexuality. It is the central feature of our humanity that enables us to give and receive life in both body and spirit. It expresses, in the most tangible sense, how we are the image and likeness of God in the power to generate life. When we think or talk about sexuality the natural inclination is always to focus on the physical expression with all its immediate pleasurable aspects. This is understandable as the whole erotic dimension of the desire for ecstatic pleasure and union with "the other" is what energises its fundamental capacity to bring new life to birth, which celebrates most beautifully the erotic yearning for unity. It is vital, however, for us to recognise the other ways in which the creative capacity to give life finds expression. Every human being has been created body and spirit, a unity of being that joins the physical and spiritual together in its capacity to give life. Love that is defined solely in terms of *eros* can very quickly degenerate into a totally physical definition of sexuality that seeks pleasurable fulfilment on its own terms and often ends up using another person simply as an object of pleasure to be discarded when necessary. It is when the new commandment, which

Jesus gave to his disciples, "Love one another as I have loved you", is taken deeply to heart that we gain a life-long context that then enables the deeper aspects of sexuality to come alive.

As we have seen it is Jesus himself who is able to slowly draw the *eros* of sexuality into an ongoing creative encounter with the power of *agape*, the love that is deeply rooted in the concern for the well-being of "the other" in all its dimensions. It is through healing the wounds that lie deeply within the core of a person's humanity that he can then bring about this new life-giving synthesis of the two fundamental ways of loving. This is only made possible when the three other dimensions of our humanity that can give life with genuine authority, namely the emotional, the psychological and the spiritual, are recognised and drawn into the process through the dynamic presence of Jesus's love.

Beginning with the emotional capacity to give life we can see this present in the formation of friendships that are lasting and have great depth, bringing alive the desire for affirmation, acceptance, intimacy and the joy that accompanies mutual commitment. When these different dimensions of friendship are present a new sense of life is generated, as a deeper level of self-acceptance can develop in a non-threatening environment. Deep friendship plays a crucial role in the reduction of aggression and fears and self-centred patterns of behaviour that prevent a real generosity of heart from growing in the depths of a person, thereby enabling a freedom of spirit to flourish.

Deep friendship also plays a crucial role in healing painful experiences of the past where rejection or casual indifference has left deep wounds that are incredibly difficult to live with, not to mention feelings of loneliness and isolation. Furthermore, attentiveness to a friend's inner world of hopes and fears can create a new spirit of optimism and creativity which can have lasting effects in all relationships with others. Deep friendship, by its very nature, always has an erotic dimension present, not necessarily physical but definitely emotional; however, a power to move beyond the normal erotic drives for pleasure, as satisfactions within themselves, is precisely the gift that comes from the heart of Jesus himself. He is the one who can take genuine friendship to the place of real sacrificial love for "the other" in a way that does not eliminate the erotic energy integral to all human attraction, but that integrates it with the self-giving love he brought alive in his death on the cross, in order to share it with us. It is precisely through the loving friendship he offers us that the deep friendships we make can be transformed, enabling the truth and beauty of another person's uniqueness to come alive in a new way.

Jesus the Healer of the Wounds of Sexuality

The suffering that Jesus underwent was accepted and indeed embraced by him in the end to free us from the wounding effects of sin that have been inherited, but also created by our own wrongdoing and disordered behaviour. As we know, the presence of sin really mutilates the emotional capacity for love and the formation of friendships, and, therefore, the healing that Jesus offers is crucial if this capacity is to be liberated, so that it can be truly life-giving.

It is not just in the emotional dimension of human sexuality that the healing power of Jesus is transformative but also, in a very particular way, in the psychological; for it is within the deeper dimension of the person that his wisdom and love can often be experienced in the most powerful ways. The human psyche, which holds the inner depths of a person, is naturally linked to the world of emotions as well as the instinctual physical drives of the body. However, it is also the gateway into that inner place where the deepest yearning to experience authentic identity, developing in its most life-giving way, resides. Unfortunately, it, too, suffers from wounds that are the consequences of genetic inheritance but also the result of painful and damaging experiences going back to the earliest days of childhood which are subsequently reinforced by other forms of conflict, both circumstantial and relational.

Now it is fair to say that everyone at some level experiences psychological conflict and pain during their lives, which can be alleviated in a number of ways. If a person is able to avail themselves of professional help the modern therapeutic world offers a variety of different methods of therapy that can be of great assistance. Different forms of counselling and long-term analytical therapy offer resources to those who are willing and financially able to work systematically with psychological issues. As has already been pointed out, friendships that have depth can often provide a context where difficult issues can be addressed, while group experiences can also enable a person to gently confront inner conflicts that otherwise would remain repressed. Sadly, however, there are many people who, for different reasons, whether personal or financial, are unable to work with their difficulties in a professional context. Hence levels of depression and other painful inner disorders, leading to compensatory addictions, self-harming and even suicide, have increased considerably in recent years. This then inevitably encourages cynicism and despair that can easily become infectious, touching the lives of others, even those who are not suffering in the same way.

The Holy Spirit in the Call to Love

Now it is Jesus who offers a relationship in which the deepest levels of darkness can be touched by his amazing love. One of the truly important developments that have taken place in recent years in many parish communities and other religious institutions is the celebration of Eucharistic Adoration, which offers a tremendous opportunity to discover the meaning of silent encounter with the living presence of the Lord Jesus. The great mystical tradition of the Church has always been one of its greatest treasures, presenting the way of contemplative prayer as a form of prayer not just for the professionally religious, but for all members of the Church, the Body of Christ, and which can, therefore, nurture the conciliar vision of the universal call to holiness. The stillness and silence in which a person can gently discover the personal *eros*, the desire, in the heart of Jesus to be at one with them is the context in which personal surrender to this love becomes the essence of prayer. This offers Jesus the opportunity to enter into the depths of a person's being, enabling him to enfold all those deepest areas of pain and anguish, uniting these with his own experience of suffering and darkness. When this takes place he can then offer his compassion and mercy in such a way that the person receiving these immense gifts is able to bestow them on others, loving them in the same way that they are being loved.

This is of particular importance in the whole area of psychological pain and conflict. Whether a person is receiving professional assistance or not, the silent encounter of Eucharistic Adoration enables Jesus to share himself uniquely with them. His compassionate love is able to sow a seed of deep desire that gently flows from a sense of identification, of being with another person in their pain, often in an unspoken way. It can then gradually become a real longing in a person to give of themselves without any desire for a response except the other person's well-being and inner healing. When this total self-giving is present, made possible as the redeeming love of Jesus comes fully alive, the Holy Spirit can then manifest his power to communicate through them to others the living presence of God's love in a unique way. This takes place because the Holy Spirit, "The Lord, the Giver of Life", is the one who enables a new identity to be born in the person who has discovered a union of love with Jesus through his healing power. This identity is that of a missionary disciple, an intimate friend of Jesus, who is inspired to share this personal experience of love in a way that brings to birth a desire in others to experience this love growing within them. It is a call to be a true witness to the power of the unitive love that they have with Jesus, which finds its fullest expression through the procreative love of the Holy Spirit working within them.

Marital Love in *Humanae Vitae*

Returning once again to *Humanae Vitae*, we can now see
clearly the importance of the presence of Jesus in the whole
experience of marital love. In the section of the encyclical
entitled "Marital Love" we see it implicitly revealing itself
in the very important aspects of love in action when Blessed
Pope Paul states:

> Above all, this love is fully *human*, that is, something
> both of the senses and spiritual. So it is a matter not of
> natural or affective instinct alone, but also, and above
> all, of an act of free will whose intention is that the love
> not only survive the joys and sorrows of daily life, but
> also grow—so that the spouses become in a way one heart
> and one soul, and can in this unity reach their human
> perfection together. [19]

In other words it is a gift of freedom that enables a couple
to move beyond the immediate demands of *eros* into that
place of total self-giving love, *agape*, in which their human
identity finds lasting fulfilment. Furthermore, it deepens
the process of growing into mutual identification through
the reality of daily experience, only made possible when
psychological conflicts are faced and begin to experience
healing, both made possible by the loving presence of Jesus.

We see this once again when Blessed Pope Paul states:

> It is a matter of a *total* love—of that special form of personal friendship in which spouses generously share everything, neither of them making unreasonable exceptions or thinking solely of his or her convenience. If one really loves one's spouse, one loves not only for what one receives but for the other's own sake; and one does this gladly, to enrich the other with one's gift of self.[20]

Here we see once again the unity of the true aspects of love, *eros* and *agape*, coming alive as the emotional aspects of sexuality find their fullest expression in the deepest form of committed friendship.

These two characteristics are the preparation for the reflection on marital love that is "*faithful* and *exclusive*, until life's end" and "is *fruitful*: it is not confined to the spouses' communion with each other; rather, it looks to extending itself and raising up new lives".[21] It is this description of love in language that implicitly connects us with the nature of Jesus's love for us – faithful and exclusive until death, a love that generates life, both physically and spiritually – that provides the powerful prelude to all the main issues that surround the transmission of life in the conjugal relationship. Blessed Pope Paul then reflects on the meaning of "Responsible Parenthood" and concludes the section with a statement that in many ways sums up the whole challenge that the encyclical presents on the human level. Referring to the married couple, he says:

From this it follows that in their role of transmitting life, spouses are not free to act just as they choose, as if they could rightly define for themselves, quite autonomously, what ways of acting are morally acceptable. On the contrary, they are bound to make their actions correspond to the design of God the Creator. a design manifested in the very nature of marriage and of marital acts, and set forth in the Church's constant teaching.[22]

The physical expression of sexuality in which erotic desires and all the immediate pleasure that fulfils them are present and active contains within it a strong tendency for omnipotent autonomy that will resist any form of challenge. Therefore, any suggestion that it must in some way be integrated into a deeper value system is likely to immediately arouse opposition and lead to rejection. However, unless the physical dimension of sexuality is integrated with the other deeper aspects, it will, in the end, lose a true sense of meaning and become purely functional, to be exercised at whim.

Proclaiming the Message of Love to Others

As the last five decades have demonstrated, the use of contraception, with all its justificatory arguments, has facilitated lifestyles and attitudes that do not promote a deeper sense of love but rather have increased the dominance of a totally self-oriented understanding of human fulfilment. Blessed Pope Paul, in the section of his encyclical entitled "Responsible Parenthood", prophetically outlines all the symptoms of this contraceptive culture which have now become commonplace and largely go unquestioned, with all the damaging consequences that have already been referred to. Unless the "design of God the Creator" is able to come alive in a way that challenges the opposition to the encyclical in a life-giving way, the true meaning of married love will continue to die, with all its tragic consequences. This is why Jesus needs to come into the centre of the picture: because he is the very embodiment of the "design of God the Creator", for he alone is the one who can activate the capacity in a person to go beyond all the dominant tendencies that exist in erotic sexuality – not by removing the presence of *eros*, but by enabling it to be integrated into the other dimensions of loving which, by their very nature, require discipline and self-sacrifice. Hence, it is his presence in the lives of married couples that then enables them to experience the unitive and procreative aspect of sexual union in a way that enhances their love for each other, infusing it with a new spirit of generosity and tenderness.

Towards the end of his encyclical Blessed Pope Paul offers pastoral directives to individuals, to those who are in positions of public authority and also particularly to members of the Church who have pastoral responsibilities. In the section on the "To Christian Spouses" he makes a very important statement in regard to married couples when he says: "The wide field of lay vocation thus comes to include a novel and outstanding kind of apostolate, in which like minister to like: couples take on an apostolic role for other married couples by becoming their guides."[23] In the light of the missionary dimension of discipleship, now at the heart of the spirit of the new evangelisation that has been developed over recent years, this statement is of particular importance in the whole presentation of the message of *Humanae Vitae*. The transmission of a truth that is lived through the dynamic presence of Jesus's love within the depth of a person's sexuality has the power to touch the lives of others in a way that can have a lasting effect on the way they live the gift of their sexuality. Recognising this truth and praying to the Holy Spirit, "the Lord, the Giver of Life", for the desire to bring it alive will be the most creative way of celebrating the 50th Anniversary of *Humanae Vitae*. It will enable Jesus to reveal himself as "The Way, the Truth and the Life" and so become "the Light of the World" in the hearts and minds of all his followers, consecrated to his love through the gift of baptism.

Endnotes

1   *2 Tm* 4:1-2.

2   *2 Tm* 4:3,5.

3   *Lumen Gentium*, Vatican Council II, The Conciliar and Post Conciliar Documents, Costello Publishing Company, 1966, p. 350.

4   Ibid., p. 396.

5   Ibid., p. 397.

6   *Mt* 5:14.

7   *Jn* 10:10.

8   Blessed Pope Paul VI, *Evangelii Nuntiandi*, CTS, London, 1975, p. 6.

9   Ibid., p. 33.

10 Pope St John Paul II, *Redemptoris Missio*, CTS, London, 1990, p. 24.

11 Pope Francis, *Evangelii Gaudium*, CTS, London, 2013, p. 10.

12 Pope St John Paul II, *Redemptoris Missio*, CTS, London, 1990, p. 90.

13 *Gaudium et Spes*, Vatican Council II, The Conciliar and Post Conciliar Documents, Costello Publishing Company, 1966, p. 914.

14 Pope Benedict XVI, *Deus Caritas Est*, CTS, London, 2006, p. 10.

15 Ibid., p. 11.

16 Ibid., p. 13.

17 Ibid., p. 15.

18 Ibid., p. 16.

19 See page 47 of this book.

20 See pp. 47-48

21 See p. 48.

22 See pp. 49-50.

23 See p. 65.

ENCYCLICAL LETTER

HUMANAE VITAE

OF THE SUPREME PONTIFF
POPE PAUL VI

TO HIS VENERABLE BROTHERS THE PATRIARCHS,
ARCHBISHOPS, BISHOPS AND OTHER LOCAL
ORDINARIES IN PEACE AND COMMUNION
WITH THE APOSTOLIC SEE, TO THE CLERGY AND
FAITHFUL OF THE WHOLE CATHOLIC WORLD,
AND TO EVERYONE OF GOOD WILL

ON REGULATING HUMAN
PROCREATION RIGHTLY

Contents

This translation was made for Catholic Truth Society for the fortieth anniversary of *Humanae Vitae* in 2008, from the Latin text, AAS 60 (1968) 481-503, by John Finnis, Professor of Law and Legal Philosophy (now Emeritus and Honorary Fellow of University College) in the University of Oxford and Fellow of the British Academy, formerly a member of the Pontifical Academy Pro Vita, of the Pontifical Council for Justice and Peace, and of the Holy See's International Theological Commission. He has supplemented it with notes about earlier English translations, about some features of this translation, and about section 16's distinction between contraception and periodic abstinence as ways of regulating procreation.

In this edition, the footnotes to the Encyclical itself will be found as endnotes, at the very end (pp. 78-80).

1. The transmitting of human life, a most serious role in which spouses share freely and responsibly in the activity of God the Creator, has always brought them great joys, and sometimes no few difficulties and deprivations.

Fulfilling this role has always raised hard questions of conscience for married people. But the changes involved in human society's recent evolution have aroused new questions, about something so closely affecting human life and happiness that they are questions the Church cannot rightly pass by.

I.
THE QUESTION'S NEW ASPECTS, AND THE MAGISTERIUM'S AUTHORITY

2. For very important changes have emerged, of various kinds. First, there is the rapid increase in births, making many fear that world population will outgrow supplies of the necessities of life, and that many families and developing countries face mounting hardship and distress–a danger which could easily tempt public authorities to opt for drastic solutions. Working and housing conditions, moreover, and the rising cost of living and expenses of raising and educating children, often make it burdensome today to provide for a large family.

Also important is a certain shift in the understanding of women's personhood and role in society, and also of the value, in marriage, of love between the spouses and the need to assess marital acts by their relationship to this love.

Finally, most important of all is mankind's amazing progress in controlling and rationally organising the forces of nature, a control now sought to extend to the whole of human life–to the human body, mental capacities and social life, and to those laws themselves that govern the generation of life.

3. From this state of things there arise new questions. Given present conditions of life, and the significance that acts of marital intercourse have for spouses' harmony and mutual fidelity, wouldn't it be appropriate to rethink the present moral norms, especially if it is felt that they cannot be adhered to without sacrifices, sometimes requiring heroic effort?

Again, applying the so-called principle of totality, couldn't it rightly be accepted that the purpose of making fecundity less prolific but more rational might transform a physically sterilizing act into a morally acceptable and provident birth control? In other words, wouldn't it be right to accept that procreation as a goal applies to the totality of married life rather than to each and every marital act? And given that people today are more aware of their responsibilities, hasn't the time come when the role of transmitting life should be entrusted to their intelligence and will rather than to their bodily rhythms?

4. Questions of this kind require from the Church's magisterium a new and deeper reflection upon the principles of the moral doctrine on marriage–a doctrine founded on natural law illuminated and enriched by divine Revelation.

No member of the faithful will deny that interpretation of natural moral law pertains to the Church's magisterium. For, as many previous Popes have said,[1] there is no doubt that when Jesus Christ made Peter and the other Apostles sharers of his divine authority and sent them to teach all nations his commandments,[2] he constituted them authentic guardians and interpreters of the whole moral law—guardians, that is, not only of the law of the Gospel but also of the natural law. For natural law, too, declares God's will, faithful submission to which is necessary for eternal salvation.[3]

In carrying out this mandate, the Church has always—and in recent times more copiously—set out consistent and appropriate teachings on the nature of marriage, the rightful use of conjugal rights, and the obligations of spouses.[4]

5. Consciousness of this teaching responsibility led me to confirm and expand the Commission set up in March, 1963 by my esteemed predecessor Pope John XXIII, which included not only many scholars in the various disciplines relevant to these questions but also married couples. This Commission's purpose was not only to examine views and opinions about questions bearing on married life, especially about rightful regulation of procreation, but also to report on the matters studied in a timely way so that the Church's magisterium might respond appropriately to the expectancy of the faithful and of people everywhere about this matter.[5]

After receiving these researches of the experts, and the opinions and advice—some unsolicited, some I had requested —of a good many of my brothers in the episcopate,

I was in a position to assess all aspects of this complex issue more thoroughly. For this I am most grateful to all concerned.

6. However, the conclusions arrived at by the Commission were not such that I could regard them as having the force of a certain and definite judgment, or as relieving me of the responsibility of considering and weighing up for myself so momentous a question. All the more so because, within the Commission itself there was no full consensus about what moral norms should be proposed; and above all because certain ways of resolving the question had emerged which were at variance with the moral doctrine on marriage which the Church's magisterium has taught with firmness and constancy.

So now, having sifted carefully the documentation sent me, having thought through the matter with most attentive mind and heart, and having prayed to God assiduously, I propose to give the grave questions indicated above a response by virtue of the mandate entrusted to me by Christ.

II.
DOCTRINAL PRINCIPLES

7. The question of procreation, like every other question touching human life, must be thought about in a way that goes beyond limited perspectives, such as the biological, psychological, demographic, or sociological. What must be considered is the whole human person, and the whole role to which he or she is called, a vocation which bears not only on natural and earthly realities but also on realities supernatural and eternal. And since many people who try to justify artificial means of restricting the number of children appeal to the demands of *marital love* and/or of *responsible parenthood*, it is necessary to clarify and accurately define these two important elements of married life. That is what I will now do, primarily by recalling what the Second Vatican Council, in its Pastoral Constitution *Gaudium et Spes*, has recently and most authoritatively taught about this matter.

Marital love

8. Marital love particularly shows us its true nature and nobility when we realise that it comes from God, its supreme source, who "is love"[6] and is the Father "from whom every parenthood in heaven and on earth takes its name."[7]

Marriage, therefore, far from originating in chance or blindly evolving natural forces, is really something wisely and providently founded by God the Creator with a view to carrying out, in human persons, his design of love. So husband and wife, through a mutual self-giving which is properly theirs and exclusive to them, develop a communion of persons by which to perfect one another so as to cooperate with God in procreating and educating new living beings.

And for those who have been baptised, marriage is endowed with the dignity of being a sacramental sign of grace, because it represents the union of Christ and the Church.

9. All this makes quite clear what marital love's characteristics and requirements are; assessing them accurately is most important.

Above all, this love is fully *human*, that is, something both of the senses and spiritual. So it is a matter not of natural or affective instinct alone, but also, and above all, of an act of free will whose intention is that the love not only survive the joys and sorrows of daily life, but also grow–so that the spouses become in a way one heart and one soul, and can in this unity reach their human perfection together.

It is a matter of a *total* love–of that special form of personal friendship in which spouses generously share everything, neither of them making unreasonable exceptions or thinking solely of his or her convenience.

If one really loves one's spouse, one loves not only for what one receives but for the other's own sake; and one does this gladly, to enrich the other with one's gift of self.

Marital love is also *faithful* and *exclusive*, until life's end. That is how husband and wife understood it on the day when, fully aware of what they were doing, they freely united themselves to one another in the bond of marriage. Though this spousal fidelity sometimes presents difficulties, no one can rightly claim it is impossible; rather, it is always honorable and rich in merit. For the example of countless married couples across the centuries proves that such fidelity not only accords with marriage's nature, but also is a spring from which flows intimate and lasting happiness.

Finally, this love is *fruitful*: it is not confined to the spouses' communion with each other; rather, it looks to extending itself and raising up new lives. "Marriage and marital love are by their nature directed toward the procreation and education of children. Children are truly the supreme gift of marriage and contribute in the highest degree to the good of their parents."[8]

Responsible parenthood

10. The spouses' love requires, therefore, that they be well aware of their role in relation to responsible parenthood, which today, for very good reason, is much insisted upon, but for the same reason needs to be understood rightly, under different inter-connected aspects.

If we look first at biological processes, responsible parenthood means an awareness of, and respect for, the functions of such processes; for in the power of procreation human reason detects biological laws that pertain to the human person.[9]

If we look next at innate drives and emotions, responsible parenthood points to the need to master them by reason and will.

If we next have regard to physical, economic, psychological and social conditions, responsible parenthood should be said to be exercised both by those who prudently and generously resolve to have more children, and by those who, for serious reasons and consistently with moral precepts, decide not to have another child, whether for a definite or an indefinite length of time.

Again, this responsible parenthood has a further aspect of paramount importance, its inner relationship to the objective moral order established by God, a true interpreter of which is right conscience. Thus the role of responsible parenthood requires the spouses to maintain a right order of priorities and acknowledge their duties toward God, themselves, their families and human society.

From this it follows that in their role of transmitting life, spouses are not free to act just as they choose, as if they could rightly define for themselves, quite autonomously, what ways of acting are morally acceptable. On the contrary, they are bound to make their actions correspond to the design of God the Creator, a design manifested in the very nature of marriage and of marital acts, and set forth in the Church's constant teaching.[10]

The two meanings or orientations of marital intercourse

11. The acts by which spouses unite with each other intimately and chastely and human life is transmitted are "morally sound and worthy", as the recent Council reiterated.[11] Nor do they cease to be legitimate when they are foreseen to be infertile by reason of causes in no way willed by the spouses; for such acts retain their orientation towards expressing and strengthening the spouses' union. As experience shows, not every act of marital intercourse results in new life. For God has arranged the laws of nature and the times of fertility wisely, so that they already, by themselves, space out successive conceptions. Still, the Church, in reminding people of the requirements of the precepts of natural law, a law interpreted by the Church's constant teaching, teaches that it is necessary that *each marital act* remain oriented in itself to the procreation of human life.[12]

12. This doctrine, often expounded by the Church's magisterium, is based on the indissoluble connection–established by God and not rightly severable by human volition–between the two inherent meanings of marital intercourse: unitive and procreative.

For marital intercourse, by its innermost structure and intelligibility, both unites husband and wife in the closest of bonds and fits them for generating new life by the working of laws inscribed in the very nature of men and women. An act of marital intercourse which preserves each essential intelligibility—union and procreation—keeps intact its meaning of mutual and true love and its orientation to parenthood, that most exalted role and vocation of man and woman. I think that men and women of our time are particularly well able to see that this doctrine accords with human reason.

13. For people rightly acknowledge that intercourse imposed by one spouse on the other, without regard to the other's condition or legitimate wishes, is not a true act of love, and so contradicts what right moral order requires of relationships between spouses. By the same token they should accept, if they think it through, that any act of mutual love which impairs the procreative power—a power that God the Creator has engraved in such acts by the working of particular laws—is an act opposed both to the divine design constitutively normative for marriage, and to the will of the Author of human life.

So if one uses this divine gift but deprives it, even partly, of its meaning and purpose, one is acting contrary to the nature of man, of woman and of their intimate relationship, and is therefore also opposing God's design and holy will.

But if one enjoys the gift of married love while respecting the laws of conception, one acknowledges that one is not master of the sources of life but rather a minister of the design established by the Creator. Just as one does not have unlimited power over one's body in general, so too, with particular reason, one has no such power over one's reproductive capacities, for these by their very nature bear on the procreation of human life, of which God is source. "For human life must be regarded by all as something sacred," recalls my predecessor Pope John XXIII, "since from its beginning it requires the action of God the Creator."[13]

Immoral ways of regulating procreation

14. On the basis, therefore, of these primary principles of the human and Christian doctrine of marriage, I must again declare that direct interruption of a generative process already begun, and above all direct abortion, even for therapeutic reasons, is to be totally rejected as a legitimate way of regulating the number of children.[14]

Equally to be condemned, as the Church's magisterium has taught repeatedly, is direct sterilization of man or woman, whether permanent or temporary.[15]

Similarly to be rejected is any act which—when marital intercourse is anticipated, being engaged in, or leading to its natural consequences—is intended (either as end or as means) to impede procreation.[16]

Nor can it rightly be asserted that the following are valid arguments to justify marital acts deliberately deprived of their fertility: that one should choose what seems the lesser evil; or that those acts coalesce with fertile acts, past or future, to form a kind of whole and so share with the fertile acts in one and the same moral goodness. For though it is true that a lesser moral evil may sometimes rightly be tolerated in order to avoid some greater evil or promote some more important good,[17] still one may never rightly–even for the most serious reasons–do evil that good may come of it,[18] that is, direct one's will to something which of its very nature violates the moral order and so must be judged unworthy of human beings, even when this is done with the purpose of protecting or promoting the good of individuals, families or human society. Consequently, it is quite mistaken to think that a marital act deliberately deprived of its fertility, and thus intrinsically immoral, could be justified by the fertile acts of intercourse in a whole married life.

Morally acceptable therapeutic measures

15. On the other hand, therapeutic measures necessary for curing physical illnesses are considered by the Church to be in no way impermissible, even if they cause an impediment to procreation, and even if that impediment is foreseen–unless it is, for whatever reason, directly intended.[19]

Moral acceptability of periodic abstinence

16. Now, as I noted earlier (sec. 3), some people today object to this doctrine of the Church about the morality governing marriage, arguing that it is human reason's right and role to control the forces which irrational nature has made available to it, and to direct them to ends appropriate for human good. Some put the argument like this: in relation to this issue, isn't it reasonable, in many circumstances, to regulate the conception of more children artificially if doing so will better serve the family's harmony and peace and provide more suitable conditions for educating children already born? To this question I must respond clearly: the Church is the first to praise and commend the use of human intelligence in an activity in which human beings, endowed with reason, are so closely associated with their Creator; but she maintains as certain that this must be done in accord with the divinely established order of things.

So when a couple have sound reasons for spacing subsequent conceptions, reasons arising from their physical or psychological condition or from external circumstances, the Church teaches that they may follow the natural cycles immanent in the reproductive system, and engage in marital intercourse only during those times when conception will not occur–and thus plan the birth of their children in a manner that in no way infringes the moral doctrine just restated.[20]

The Church is consistent with herself and her teaching, both in judging that spouses may rightly have recourse to infertile times, and in condemning the use of means to directly impede conception as always wrong even when the reasons given for this use seem morally sound and serious. For these two approaches to birth regulation really differ from each other greatly: in the former, the spouses make legitimate use of an opportunity made available to them by nature; in the latter they impede the natural processes of reproduction. If it is undeniable that in both cases the spouses definitely are mutually agreed in wanting, for acceptable reasons, to avoid children and to make sure that none are likely to come, it is equally undeniable that only in the former is it the case that the spouses [i] are strong in abstaining from intercourse during the fertile period, whenever procreating children is for sound reasons undesirable, and then, when infertile times come round again, [ii] engage in intercourse to express their mutual love and maintain their promised commitment to each other. By this whole course of conduct, these spouses give real witness to a love that is truly and integrally right.

Consequences of accepting immoral methods

17. Good people can become more fully convinced of the truth of the doctrine which the Church teaches on this issue, if they think about what will follow from the ways and means proposed for limiting births by technical

measures. They will first reflect how wide and easy is the road this policy opens up, both to marital infidelity and to a general decay of morals. Nor does one need long experience to be fully aware of human weakness and to understand that human beings—and especially the young, so subject to desires—need incentives to keep the moral law, and ought not to be offered an easy way to violate it. It is greatly to be feared, too, that men grown used to contraceptive methods will become unmindful of reverence for women—that, disregarding the woman's physical and emotional equilibrium, the man will make of her his instrument in the service of his self-centred desire, no longer regarding her as a companion owed ongoing respect and love.

It should be carefully considered, finally, how dangerous is the power this would concede to public authorities that have scant concern for the precepts of the moral law. Who will blame a government for tackling its nation's problems with measures of the kind claimed to be morally permissible for married people to solve some family problem? Who will prevent public authorities from favoring the ways of preventing conception they think more effective, or indeed from ordering everyone to use them whenever the authorities think necessary? In this way people, anxious to avoid difficulties associated with divine law—difficulties they experience as individuals, families or social groups—may come to surrender to public authorities the power to intervene at will in the married couple's most private and intimate role.

So unless we want responsibility for procreating life to be handed over to human discretion, we must acknowledge that the power one can have over one's own body and its natural functions has some limits beyond which it is wrong to go, limits which no one, whether private individual or public authority, can rightly transgress. These limits are established precisely out of the reverence which is owed to the whole human organism and its natural functions, according to the principles I have recalled above, and a right understanding of the "principle of totality" enunciated by my predecessor Pope Pius XII.[21]

18. It can be foreseen that not everyone perhaps will easily accept this teaching, for too many voices, magnified by the modern media, are raised in discord with the voice of the Church. But the Church–unsurprised to find herself destined, like her divine Founder, to be a "sign of contradiction"[22]– does not use this as ground for evading the duty imposed on her of proclaiming humbly but firmly the whole moral law, the natural law as well as the law of the Gospel.

Since the Church did not make either of these laws, she cannot be their arbiter, but only their guardian and interpreter. It could never be right for her to declare morally permissible what in truth is morally impermissible, since that is always by its very nature opposed to authentic human good.

In preserving intact the whole moral law of marriage, the Church well knows that she is making a contribution to renewing a true human civilization. She urges men and women not to entrust themselves so far to technical means that they abdicate their personal responsibilities. And all this she does to defend the dignity of husband and wife. By doing so, the Church, loyal to the example and teaching of the divine Savior, shows that she accompanies men and women with a sincere and generous love, even on this their earthly journey, striving to help them "share as sons and daughters in the life of the living God, the Father of all mankind".[23]

III.

PASTORAL DIRECTIVES AND APPEALS

19. My words would not adequately express the thoughts and solicitude of the Church, Mother and Teacher of all peoples, unless–having urged the keeping and fostering of God's law on marriage–they also supported men and women in moral ways of regulating the number of their children in the difficult conditions pressing families and nations today. For the Church cannot behave towards people except as the divine redeemer did, knowing their weakness, having compassion on the multitude, and welcoming sinners. Yet she can do no other than teach the law which really belongs to human lives restored to their authentic truth and led by God's Spirit.[24]

20. The Church's teaching on rightly regulating procreation promulgates divine law, but keeping to it will undoubtedly seem to many not just difficult but impossible. And like all outstandingly noble and beneficial goods, this law does indeed require of individuals, families and human society a resolute purpose and many efforts. In fact, it cannot be kept save with the help of God's grace, which sustains and strengthens human good wills. Yet it will be evident to all who consider the matter carefully that those same

efforts enhance the dignity of men and women and benefit human society.

21. Morally right and proper birth regulation requires of spouses that they profoundly appreciate the true goods of life and family, and that they become accustomed to controlling themselves and their desires completely. To govern natural drives by reason and free will, so that the expressions of love which belong to married life will be morally in order, undoubtedly requires self-denial–*ascesis*–a governance of instinct particularly required for the practice of periodic abstinence from intercourse. Far from hindering the spouses' love for one another, this self-discipline, shining witness to their purity, imbues the love with greater human meaning. It needs a persevering resolve, but the strength it gives their characters enables spouses to develop themselves fully and enriches them with spiritual goods: for [i] it brings family life abundant fruits of tranquility and peace, and helps solve difficulties of other kinds; [ii] in each of the spouses it fosters care and consideration for the other; [iii] it helps them drive out selfishness, true charity's enemy, and stimulates awareness of their responsibilities. Finally, [iv] it gives parents a deeper and more effective influence in the education of children who as they grow through childhood and adolescence have a sound understanding of true human goods and use their powers of mind and sense serenely and appropriately.

22. I wish to take this opportunity to remind educators, and all whose right and duty it is to provide for human society's common good, that they need to usher in a state of affairs favourable to cultivating chastity, so that true liberty, fully respecting moral norms, may prevail over license. Everything in today's media which is sensually arousing and fosters dissolute morals, and likewise all kinds of obscenity in the written word or licentious films or theatrical productions, should therefore be condemned publicly and with united voice by all who are interested in promoting civilization or safeguarding the human spirit's most important goods. To try to defend these depravities by arguments from the arts or learning[25] or by pleading the freedom which public authorities sometimes allow in this domain, would be wrong-headed.

To rulers of nations

23. I appeal, therefore, to national rulers, who bear supreme responsibility for safeguarding the common good, and who can contribute so much to the preservation of morals: that they may never allow the morals of their peoples to be ruined. They should in no way allow laws to introduce into the family–the primary element in the state– practices opposed to natural and divine law. For there is another way by which civil authority can and should solve the problem of rising population: legislating prudently for families, and educating their peoples wisely enough to safeguard moral law and citizens' freedom alike.

I am fully aware how difficult this whole issue is for governments, especially in the developing countries. And it was with their reasonable anxieties in mind that I issued my encyclical *Populorum Progressio*. But now I reiterate what Pope John XXIII said: "Those problems must be solved without resort to means or schemes contrary to human dignity, such as are proposed by people who think that human beings and human life are nothing but matter. All this can only be solved, we believe, if economic and social development is in the service of individual citizens and the whole of human society alike, and promotes authentic goods."[26] And it would be a libel to blame divine Providence for what evidently results rather from unwise governmental policies, a feeble sense of social justice, the accumulating of material goods for selfish gain, and a sluggish neglect to make the efforts and sacrifices needed to raise the standard of living of peoples and their children.[27] Would that all governments concerned would do what some are already doing so admirably, and bestir themselves to renew their undertakings and efforts! There should be no slackening in willingness to give mutual aid to all parts of the great human family: here there lies open an almost limitless field, I believe, for the great international organisations to do their work.

To scientists

24. I wish next to address some words of encouragement to scientists, who "can greatly benefit marriage and the

family, and the peace of consciences, if by coordinated researches they seek a deeper understanding of the various conditions favorable to regulating human procreation in a morally acceptable way."[28] Pre-eminently to be desired, as Pius XII indicated some time ago, is success in medically establishing a secure enough basis for regulating birth in a morally acceptable way by observation of the natural cycles.[29] The work of scientists, especially Catholics, will in this way demonstrate that, as the Church teaches, "there can be no real contradiction between divine law on transmitting life and divine law on nurturing authentic marital love."[30]

To Christian spouses

25. My words are now addressed more especially to my own sons and daughters, and most of all to those whom God calls to serve him in the state of matrimony. For the Church, while handing on divine law's inviolable requirements, is also proclaiming salvation and through the sacraments is opening up channels of the grace by which one is made a new creature, responds in charity and true freedom to the design of one's Creator and Savior, and finds sweet the yoke of Christ.[31]

In seemly compliance, therefore, with her voice, Christian spouses are mindful that their vocation to a Christian life, a vocation springing from baptism, has been further specified and confirmed by the sacrament of marriage–by which they are "fortified and receive a kind of consecration" so that they may fulfil their role with fidelity, realise their vocation to the full, and bear Christian witness, as becomes them, before the world.[32] For the Lord has entrusted them with this role so that they may make visible to others the holiness and sweetness of a law by which their love for each other is closely united to their cooperation with God's love–love in and from the very author of human life.

I have no wish to leave unspoken the difficulties, sometimes grave, encountered in the lives of Christian spouses. For them as for each of us, "the gate is narrow and the way is hard that leads to life."[33] Still, hope for that life should illumine their journey like the brightest of lights, while they strive with fortitude to "live sober, upright and godly lives in this world,"[34] sure in the knowledge that "the form of this world is passing away."[35]

So husbands and wives should willingly take up the tasks assigned them, strengthened by faith and by the hope which "does not disappoint us, because God's love has been poured into our hearts through the Holy Spirit who has been given to us."[36] With persistent prayer they should implore divine assistance, and should especially draw from that unfailing well of grace and charity, the Eucharist. If, however, sins keep hold of them, they should not lose heart, but have humble and persevering recourse to God's mercy, abundantly bestowed in the sacrament of Penance.

In this way they will be able to reach perfection of married life, which the Apostle describes thus: "Husbands, love your wives, as Christ loved the Church... Even so husbands should love their wives as their own bodies. He who loves his wife loves himself. For no man ever hates his own flesh, but nourishes and cherishes it, as Christ does the Church... This is a great mystery, and I mean in reference to Christ and the Church; however, let each one of you love his wife as himself, and let wives respect their husbands."[37]

26. One of the most important of the fruits which ripen when divine law is kept with resolution is the desire of a good many married couples to communicate their own experience to others. The wide field of lay vocation thus comes to include a novel and outstanding kind of apostolate, in which like minister to like: couples take on an apostolic role for other married couples by becoming their guides. Among so many forms of Christian apostolate, this seems one most opportune today.[38]

To healthcare professionals

27. Similarly most estimable, too, are those doctors and other healthcare workers who in performing their role are concerned to carry out what is required of them by the specific meaning of a Christian vocation, rather than by any sort of human utility. May they, therefore, persevere with constant intent always to favour solutions conformable to faith and right reason; and may they strive to win

from their professional colleagues assent and respect for these solutions.

They should regard it as a part of their professional role to acquire all the knowledge necessary to be fully proficient in this difficult field, so that when married couples ask their opinion, they can give them the right advice and point them in the proper direction, as such couples quite rightly expect of them.

To Priests

28. And now, dear sons who are priests, and who in the sacred role you exercise act as counselors and spiritual guides for individuals and families, I speak to you filled with confidence. For it is your principal responsibility– I address especially you who teach moral theology–to state the Church's teaching on marriage completely and with clarity. In the performance of your ministry, be the first to exemplify that sincere assent which should inwardly and outwardly be accorded to the magisterium of the Church. For you know that you owe it such assent by reason not so much of the arguments put forward, as of that light of the Holy Spirit which the Church's pastors, particularly, enjoy in expounding the truth.[39] You are aware, too, that it is of the utmost importance for preserving the peace of souls and the unity of the Christian people that in morals as much as in dogmatics all should comply with the Church's magisterium and speak with one voice.

Wherefore, making my own the anxious words of the great Apostle Paul and with all my heart I again appeal to you: "I appeal to you, brethren, by the name of our Lord Jesus Christ, that all of you agree and that there be no dissensions among you, but that you be united in the same mind and the same judgement."[40]

29. To omit nothing from the saving doctrine of Christ is a pre-eminent form of charity toward souls, but should always be joined with the tolerance and charity that Christ himself exemplified in speaking and dealing with men and women. For since he had come not to judge, but to save the world,[41] he was pungently severe about sin but patient and merciful toward sinners.

So in the priest's words and heart, husbands and wives cast down by their problems should find a kind of likeness of our Redeemer's voice and love.

Speak with full confidence, beloved sons, convinced that the Holy Spirit of God is present to the magisterium proclaiming sound doctrine and at the same time illumines from within the hearts of the faithful and invites them to assent. Teach married couples the necessary way of prayer, and fittingly prepare them so that they more often and with great faith receive the sacraments of the Eucharist and Penance and are never discouraged by their own weakness.

To Bishops

30. Reaching the end of this encyclical, my mind now turns reverently and lovingly to you my beloved and venerable brothers in the episcopate, with whom I share more closely the care of the spiritual good of the People of God. I urge on you all this pressing request: that, leading both the priests who assist in your sacred ministry and the faithful in your dioceses, you devote yourselves promptly and with all zeal to protecting marriage and keeping it holy, so that conjugal life may attain its human and Christian perfection. Look upon this role as greatest among the works and burdens at present entrusted to you. For as you well know, it is a role calling for concerted pastoral action in every field of human activity, economic, cultural and social. If simultaneous progress is made in all these fields, with fidelity to the design that God conceived for the world, the inner family life of parents and children will become more tolerable but also easier and more joyful, and the various forms of human association will be enriched with fraternal charity and made more secure in true peace.

To all

31. Venerable brothers, beloved sons, all men and women of good will, great indeed is the work of education, development and charity to which I am summoning you, relying as I do upon the Church's constant and most firm teaching, which Peter's successor together with his

brothers in the Catholic episcopate faithfully guards and interprets. This truly great work, I am convinced, is to the benefit of the world and of the Church; for the true happiness to which men and women aspire with all their capacities of soul cannot be attained without adhering to the laws inscribed in their very nature by almighty God, laws whose living out is a work of practical reason and of love. On this great work, on all of you, and especially on married couples, I implore from God most holy and merciful the abundance of heavenly graces, in pledge of which I gladly give my Apostolic blessing.

Given at St Peter's, Rome, on the feast of St James the Apostle, 25th July 1968, in the sixth year of my pontificate.

PAUL VI

NOTES ON EARLIER TRANSLATIONS

When *Humanae Vitae* was published at the end of July 1968, the Holy See issued translations in major modern languages. These, including the English translation published in *L'Osservatore Romano*, weekly English edition, 1st August 1968, were evidently derived from the Italian and/or French versions, not the Latin. That English version was evidently felt to be in some ways too close to Italian idiom, and/or not close enough to the Latin. Accordingly, the Catholic Truth Society published in September 1968 a translation by Bishop Alan C. Clark and Fr Geoffrey Crawfurd "from the Latin text". A revised version of this was published by the CTS in 1970 and has been reissued by the CTS from time to time down to 2007. Meanwhile, however, a different revision of the Clark-Crawfurd translation had been published in the United States in 1969 in *The Pope Speaks* 13 (1969) 329-46, and it is this version which is to be found on the Vatican website in 2008. All these versions are essentially revisions of the Holy See's 1968 English version, made to bring the latter more into line with the Latin.

Quotations from *Humanae Vitae* in the Holy See's English versions of subsequent papal documents, notably in Pope John Paul II's Apostolic Exhortation on the Christian Family in the Modern World, *Familiaris Consortio*, 22nd

November 1981, have been made from the Holy See's 1968 English. An exception is the *Catechism of the Catholic Church* (1993, revised ed. 1997), which was done into English from the original French text and therefore, when it quotes *Humanae Vitae*, does so by translating directly from the Holy See's French version of 1968.

NOTES ON THIS TRANSLATION

Titles: "Birth Control" and "On Regulating Human Procreation Rightly": *de propagatione humanae prolis recte ordinanda*: CTS 1968 "The Right Ordering of the Procreation of Children"; the Holy See's 1968 translation, like the Italian, Spanish, etc., says "On the Regulation of Birth"; the announcement of the encyclical's publication in *L'Osservatore Romano* English edition, 1st August 1968, speaks of "the question of birth-control" and, later, "means of birth-control".

Part I: 'The question's new aspects, and the Magisterium's authority': like the other titles and headings and the table of contents, this is not part of the Latin text. The Holy See's modern language versions of 1968 have titles for the three parts, as here, and headings for sections, varying from one version to another. In this translation, the headings are reduced in number and chosen by the present translator.

"The Church's authority": the Holy See's English translation of 1968 says "competency", corresponding to Italian "competenza" and equivalent French and Spanish terms, for which however the more proper English is authority (rightful power to address the matter).

Section 1: "role": *munus*, a Latin word used over 250 times by the Second Vatican Council (1962-65), with a range of meanings such as role, mission, responsibility, and gift. The Italian and other modern language versions issued by the Holy See in 1968 use *dovere*, duty, in this and some other sections. In sections 10 and 17, on the other hand, *munus* clearly means "function", Italian "funzione".

Section 2: "women's personhood": *mulieris persona*; Spanish "la personalidad de la mujer"; Italian "la persona della donna".

Section 4: "consistent and appropriate teachings": *congrua documenta*. The Italian is "adeguato insegnamento", Spanish "una doctrina coherente", French "un enseignement cohérente".

"on the rightful use of conjugal rights": *de recto coniugum iurium usu*, that is, on the moral issues involved in seeking and engaging in marital intercourse.

Section 5: "me", "my", "I": the document uses throughout the formal expressions "Us", "Our", "We", and related formalities, customary until the pontificate of John Paul II.

Section 7: "human person", "his and her": the document generally uses *homo*, Latin for man (or mankind) as a species; the Latin for a man in the sense of a male is *vir*, and English lacks this distinction. Section 10.2 uses *humana persona* to refer to what section 7 calls *homo*.

Section 8: "marital love": *coniugalis amor*, "conjugal love", "married love", "love in marriage". The document throughout uses *coniugalis*, and similarly uses *coniuges*, "spouses", "married people", "married couple(s)", "husband and wife". In sec. 9.4 the Latin uses *sponsus et sponsa* and in sec. 12.2 *maritum et uxorem*, terms for husband and wife. The Latin uses *maritalis* on two or three occasions as synonym for *coniugalis*, when speaking of intercourse.

"parenthood": *paternitas*, Greek *patria*, "fatherhood"; Holy See's English translation 1968, following Revised Standard Version, "family".

Section 9: "something both of the senses and spiritual": *sensibilis et spiritualis*.

Section 10: "responsible parenthood": *paternitas conscia*; Italian "paternità responsabile", French "paternité responsible"; Holy See's English translation 1968 "'responsible parenthood'".

"biological laws that pertain to the human person": *biologicas leges, quae ad humanam personam pertinent*: Italian "leggi biologiche che riguardano la persona umana"; French "lois biologiques qui font partie de la personne humaine".

"keep a right order of priorities": *rerum bonorumque ordine recte servato*; Italian "in una giusta gerarchia dei valori"; French "dans une juste hiérarchie des valeurs".

Section 11: "morally sound and worthy": *honesti ac digni*; Italian "onesti e degni".

"orientation", "oriented": *destinatio, destinatus*: CTS 1968 "natural adaptation"…"natural potential". The Holy See's modern language translations, too, do not retain the parallelism between these two sentences, but use (Italian) "ordinati ad" etc. in the first and "aperto" [open] in the second. The phrase *apertus ad novam vitam* ["open to new life"] is used by the Synod of Bishops in 1980 in solemnly reaffirming *Humanae Vitae* sec. 11; see likewise Pope John Paul II's Apostolic Exhortation *Familiaris Consortio* (1981), sec. 29 (also sec. 32.4). Sec. 14 establishes the meaning of "oriented" and "open" alike: orientation or openness to procreation is what is annulled, or not preserved, when something is done with intent to impede the procreativity of an act of spousal intercourse because it is thought that it might result in procreation.

Section 12: "its innermost structure and intelligibility… each essential intelligibility": *intimam suam rationem… essentialis ratio*; Holy See's English translation 1968 "its intimate structure…essential aspects"; Italian "sua intima struttura…aspetti essenziali"; CTS 1968 "fundamental structure…essential qualities".

"orientation": *ordinem*; Italian "ordinamento". Like the present translation, the German version approved by the German bishops uses the same word to translate *destinatus* in sec. 11 and *ordo* in sec. 12 ["hingeordnet/Hinordnung"].

"accords with human reason": *humanae rationi consentanea*; Holy See's English translation 1968 "the deeply reasonable and human character of"; Italian "consentanea alla ragione umana"; French "le caractère profondément raisonnable et humain de".

Section 14: "is intended (as end or means) to": *id, tamquam finem obtinendum aut viam adhibendam, intendat ut*; Italian "si proponga, come scopo o come mezzo, di".

76

"impede": *impedire*; Italian "impedire"; French "rendre impossible"; Holy See's English translation 1968 and *Catechism of the Catholic Church* 2370 "render impossible"; CTS 1968 "prevent". In Italian "impedire" can mean prevent or obstruct/impede/hinder; but in Latin *impedire* means obstruct/impede/hinder, and it is *prohibere* that means prevent or make impossible.

Section 15: "physical illnesses": *morbos corporis*; Italian "malattie dell'organismo"; Holy See's English translation 1968 "diseases of the organism"; CTS 1968 "organic diseases".

Section 16: "two approaches to birth regulation": *duae causae*; Italian "due casi"; Holy See's English translation 1968 and CTS 1968 "two cases".

"impede the natural processes of reproduction": *impediunt, quominus generationis ordo suos habeat naturae processus*; Italian "impediscono lo svolgimento dei processi naturali"; Holy See's English translation 1968 "impede the development of natural processes"; CTS 1968 "obstruct the natural development of the generative process". These differences of formulation do not affect the moral position developed in the encyclical. For as secs. 11, 12 and 13 have explained (presupposing secs. 8, 9 and 10, and following *Gaudium et spes* 51), the moral point is not that natural processes should never be impeded; nor, as sec. 15 has made clear, is it that the processes of a human reproductive system should never be deliberately altered or subjected to techniques or "artificial" methods. The moral point is rather that such an intervention is wrong when choosing to make it is choosing to deprive an act of intercourse (foreseen, present or past) of its expressiveness of marriage's and marital love's procreativeness–that is, is choosing to deprive that act of intercourse of its orientation or openness to procreation, its "procreative meaning" [one of the two meanings that, if intercourse is to be truly marital–enabling the spouses to express, experience and actualize their marriage–must each be preserved and never separated]. There is inevitably such a deliberate deprivation of procreative meaning or expressiveness whenever husband or wife do something to impede an act of intercourse from having the generative outcome to which (they believe) *that act* would or might otherwise have led by natural processes. Willingness to do this is indeed an approach to birth regulation quite different in moral character from the approach of those who, though similarly having good reason not to procreate, are unwilling to deprive any of their acts of intercourse of procreative meaning or expressiveness, and so instead abstain from intercourse when they think its natural outcome would or might be conception.

Endnotes

[1] See Pius IX, encyc. letter *Qui pluribus: Pii IX P.M. Acta*, 1, pp. 9-10; St Pius X encyc. letter *Singulari quadam*: AAS 4 (1912), 658; Pius XI, encyc. letter *Casti connubii*: AAS 22 (1930), 579-581; Pius XII, address *Magnificate Dominum* to the episcopate of the Catholic World: AAS 46 (1954), 671-672; *John* XXIII, encyc. letter *Mater et Magistra*: AAS 53 (1961), 457.

[2] See *Mt* 28:18-19.

[3] See *Mt* 7:21.

[4] See Council of Trent Roman Catechism, Part II, ch. 8; Leo XIII, encyc. letter *Arcanum*: *Acta Leonis XIII*, 2 (1880), 26-29; Pius XI, encyc. letter *Divini illius Magistri*: AAS 22 (1930), 58-61; encyc. letter *Casti connubii*: AAS 22 (1930), 545-546; Pius XII, Address to Italian Medico-Biological Union of St Luke: *Discorsi e radiomessaggi di Pio XII*, VI, 191-192; to Italian Association of Catholic Midwives: AAS 43 (1951), 835-854; to the association known as the Family Campaign, and other family associations: AAS 43 (1951), 857-859; to 7th congress of International Society of Hematology: AAS 50 (1958), 734-735; John XXIII, encyc. letter *Mater et Magistra*: AAS 53 (1961), 446-447; Second Vatican Council, Pastoral Constitution on the Church in the World of Today, nos. 47-52: AAS 58 (1966), 1067-1074; Code of Canon Law, canons 1067, 1068 §1, canon 1076, §§1-2.

[5] See Paul VI, Address to Sacred College of Cardinals: AAS 56 (1964), 588; to Commission for the Study of Problems of Population, Family and Birth: AAS 57 (1965), 388; to National Congress of the Italian Society of Obstetrics and Gynecology: AAS 58 (1966), 1168.

[6] See 1 *Jn* 4:8.

[7] *Eph* 3:15.

[8] Second Vatican Council, Pastoral Constitution on the Church in the World of Today, *Gaudium et spes*, no. 50: AAS 58 (1966), 1070-1072.

[9] See St Thomas, *Summa Theologiae*, I-II, q. 94, art. 2.

[10] See Second Vatican Council, Pastoral Constitution on the Church in the World of Today, *Gaudium et spes*, nos . 50-51: AAS 58 (1966) 1070-1073.

[11] See *ibid.*, no. 49: AAS 58 (1966), 1070.

[12] See Pius XI. encyc. letter *Casti connubii*: AAS 22 (1930), 560; Pius XII, Address to Midwives: AAS 43 (1951), 843.

[13] See encyc. letter *Mater et Magistra*: AAS 53 (1961), 447.

[14] See Council of Trent Roman Catechism, Part II, ch. 8; Pius XI, encyc. letter *Casti connubii*: AAS 22 (1930), 562-564; Pius XII, Address to Medico-Biological Union of St Luke: *Discorsi e radiomessaggi*, VI, 191-192; Address to Midwives: AAS 43 (1951), 842-843; Address to Family Campaign and other family associations: AAS 43 (1951), 857-859; John XXIII, encyc. letter *Pacem in terris*: AAS 55 (1963), 259-250; Second Vatican Council, Pastoral Constitution on the Church in the World of Today, *Gaudium et spes*, no. 51: AAS 58 (1966), 1072.

[15] See Pius XI, encyc. letter *Casti connubii*: AAS 22 (1930), 565; Decree of the Holy Office, 22nd Feb, 1940: AAS 32 (1940), 73; Pius XII, Address to Midwives: AAS 43 (1951) 843-844; to the Society of Hematology: AAS 50 (1958), 734-735.

[16] See Council of Trent Roman Catechism, Part II, ch. 8; Pius XI, encyc. letter *Casti connubii*: AAS 22 (1930), 559-561; Pius XII, Address to Midwives: AAS 43 (1951), 843; to the Society of Hematology: AAS 50 (1958), 734-735; John XXIII, encyc. letter *Mater et Magistra*: AAS 53 (1961), 447.

[17] See Pius XII, Address to National Congress of Italian Society of the Union of Catholic Jurists: AAS 45 (1953), 798-799.

[18] See *Rm* 3:8.

[19] See Pius XII, Address to 26th Congress of Italian Association of Urology: AAS 45 (1953), 674-675; to Society of Hematology: AAS 50 (1958), 734-735.

[20] See Pius XII, Address to Midwives: AAS 43 (1951), 846.

[21] See Pius XII, Address to Association of Urology: AAS 45 (1953), 674-675; to leaders and members of Italian Association of Cornea Donors and Italian Association for the Blind: AAS 48 (1956), 461-462.

[22] *Lk* 2:34.

[23] See Paul VI, encyc. letter *Populorum progressio*: AAS 59 (1967), 268.

80

[24] See *Rm* 8.

[25] See Second Vatican Council, Decree on the Media of Social Communication, *Inter mirifica*, nos. 6-7: AAS 56 (1964), 147.

[26] Encyc. letter *Mater et Magistra*: AAS 53 (1961), 447.

[27] See encyc. letter *Populorum progressio*, nos. 48-55: AAS 59 (1967), 281-284.

[28] Second Vatican Council, Pastoral Constitution on the Church in the World of Today, *Gaudium et spes*, no. 52: AAS 58 (1966), 1074.

[29] Address to Family Campaign and other family associations: AAS 43 (1951), 859.

[30] Second Vatican Council, Pastoral Constitution on the Church in the World of Today, *Gaudium et spes*, no. 51: AAS 58 (1966), 1072.

[31] See *Mt* 11:30.

[32] See Second Vatican Council, Pastoral Constitution on the Church in the World of Today, *Gaudium et spes*, no. 48 [from which the words quoted in this sentence are taken]: AAS 58 (1966), 1067-1069; Dogmatic Constitution on the Church, *Lumen gentium*, no. 35: AAS 57 (1965), 40-41.

[33] *Mt* 7:14; see *Heb* 12:11.

[34] See *Titus* 2:12.

[35] See *1 Cor* 7:31.

[36] *Rm* 5:5.

[37] *Eph* 5:25, 28-29, 32-33.

[38] See Second Vatican Council, Dogmatic Constitution on the Church, *Lumen gentium*, nos. 35, 41: AAS 57 (1965), 40-45; Pastoral Constitution on the Church in the World of Today, *Gaudium et spes*, nos. 48-49: AAS 58 (1966), 1067-1070; Decree on the Apostolate of the Laity, *Apostolicam actuositatem*, no. 11: AAS 58 (1966), 847-849.

[39] See Second Vatican Council, Dogmatic Constitution on the Church, *Lumen gentium*, no. 25: AAS 57 (1965), 29-31.

[40] *1 Cor* 1:10.

[41] See *Jn* 3:17.

Fr Anthony Doe, ordained in 1981, is a priest of the diocese of Westminster, and is currently the Spiritual Director at the Venerable English College in Rome. He is also a trained psychotherapist and has a Master's Degree in Psychology of Religion and a Doctoral Thesis on the Development of Self Identity based on a dialogue between the psychoanalyst Donald Winnicott and the teachings of St John of the Cross.

Cover image: *A couple and sunrise.* | © Shutterstock.com

HOLY DAYS

LITTLE WORKBOOK

INTRODUCTORY NOTE

This workbook is based on its companion volume, HOLY DAYS: THE LITURGICAL YEAR IN PRACTICE, but provides more space for noting local/personal additions. It can be used independently, but does assume familiarity with (or access to) certain basics set forth in the book. For more elaborate details and further explanations, see the book itself – occasional references (to notes, tables etc, given in the book) are marked: *HD*.

   NB: Within the ancient Orthodox Tradition there exists a truly remarkable and heart-warming unity – throughout the centuries, and all over the world. At the same time, however, one should be aware that the life of the Church is lived in the reality of this world, with real people, in real communities – each with their own character and special qualities, as well as inevitable human limitations. Therefore, *please note that all details concerning commemorations, services 'commonly celebrated', special dispensations etc, are subject to local practice as well as practical limitations* – which, of necessity, may vary even within a particular jurisdiction.

And of His fulness have all we received,
and grace for grace ... (Jn.1)

HOLY DAYS: LITTLE WORKBOOK
A title in the series: Living the Orthodox Calendar
AD 2024 © A. Arnold-Lyklema
Published by: Maranatha House (.info)
ISBN: 978-1-917556-01-9

Companion volume of the book, 'Holy Days: the Liturgical Year in Practice' (978-1-917556-00-2)

PLEASE, RETURN THIS BOOK
To:

Contact
details:

IN CASE OF EMERGENCIES
Please contact:

LIST OF ABBREVIATIONS

In general, the Orthodox calendar has been remarkably stable throughout the centuries. The basic calendar is shared by all, and includes Saints from all the ancient Orthodox Christian Churches. Variants in the main celebration for the day usually result from later additions related to local saints (major variants have been noted). The Slav Tradition (SLV) covers a wide area which includes several of the local Orthodox Churches, some of which also have their own particular customs.

General

(IC) XC	(Jesus) Christ
...-for-XC	for Christ's sake
Bl.	Blessed
Rgt	Righteous
St, Sts	Saint, Saints
Vn	Venerable

Hierarchs / Clergy

Archbp(s)	Archbishop(s)
Archim.	Archimandrite
Bp(s)	Bishop(s)
Dcn	Deacon
Metr	Metropolitan
Patr	Patriarch
Pr	Priest

Place names

Alx'a	Alexandria
C'ple	Constantinople
Jer.	Jerusalem
Thess.	Thessalonica

Martyrs

Conf.	Confessor(s)
Mrt	Martyr(s)
GtM	Great-martyr

HrM	Hieromartyr
NwM	New-martyr
VgM	Virgin-martyr
WnM	Woman-martyr
& comp	& companions

Various

Ap	Apostle(s)
Ap(12/70)	... of the 12/70
ApEv	Ap & Evangelist
Ath	Athonite, Mt Athos
EqAp	Equal-to-the-Ap's
Proph	Prophet
Unmerc	Unmercenary Physician(s)
Wonderw	Wonderworker(s)

Local usage

BU	Bulgarian
CY	Cypriot
EL	Greek
GE	Georgian
KY	Cypriot-Athonite
SE	Serbian
SLV	Slav/Slavonic
RO	Romanian

OC/NC = Old/New Calendar

HOW TO USE THIS WORKBOOK

A FEW SUGGESTIONS

In the traditional setting, simply participating in the life of the local community of the faithful introduces us into the life-giving riches of the Orthodox Tradition – and how to understand it, how to live it, and how to make it our own. Practical use of the calendar may serve the same purpose.

♦ **Prepare a liturgical diary:** Use the book (*HD*) for general reference, and customize this workbook for the current/coming year. (Option: make this a yearly habit.)

♦ **Create your own reference book,** as a personal companion to *HD* (any year): Add local and/or newly canonized saints, personal dates and memorable events

♦ **Share either of the above with others:** as a little project for a study-group, catechism, or home-school. (Note, that the same can also be done with the book itself.)

HOW TO CUSTOMIZE THE CALENDAR FOR A PARTICULAR YEAR

To prepare this workbook for a particular year, *first choose which calendar to follow (OC/NC)*. Then find the details for the following calendar elements. Page margins can be used to note the appropriate date or weekday, next to each entry (for greater clarity, some like to use a different colour for the Sundays – e.g. red for Sundays, black for other weekdays).

Ask for the old paths, where is the good way, and walk therein, and ye shall find rest for your souls. + Jer.6:16 (KJV)

1) The Date for the Sunday of Pascha (p.110)

The structure of the liturgical year is centred on the celebration of Pascha (Easter). The tables on the following pages give the Orthodox date of Pascha for every year of the 21st century, based on the ancient Paschalion – noting both the OC date (Julian calendar/ Old Style) and the equivalent civil date (used also by those on NC). Alternatively, one can use a simple formula to find this most crucial date – *see p.14 (same as HD, p.234).*

2) Sundays of the Paschal Cycle (p.8 & p.84-ff)

From the date of Pascha we can derive all other dates of the Paschal cycle (Triodion & Pentecostarion). In general, it is helpful, first of all, to mark all the Sundays of this period. Once we have entered those dates, we can easily fill in the dates for the remaining weekdays – which completes this section of the calendar. [*To make this step even easier, see HD (p.197-ff) for a convenient reference to these Sundays and a few other crucial dates, already worked out for all possible dates of Pascha.*]

3) Linking the Paschal Cycle to the Menaion:

For easy transition, it is helpful to note, *a)* the beginning of the Triodion on the appropriate date in the Menaion section (which will fall somewhere in Jan/Feb), and *b)* the end of the Pentecostarion (Sunday of All Saints, in May/Jun - Jun/Jul).

4) Sundays during the Menaion (p.19-ff)

All dates are marked with one of seven letters, *as set forth on p.9 (and in HD, p.191)*, which enables us to find the weekday for any date – as well as the letter-equivalent for the Sunday, which remains the same from 1 Mar until 28/29 Feb.

Thus, we can easily mark the Sundays for the entire year, as follows: *a)* Find the Sunday letter for Pascha, and mark the Sundays from March 1st onwards. Then, *b)* find the Sunday letter for the previous Year/Pascha, for the Sundays before March. *(NB: The present difference between OC/NC is 13 days, so the letter-equivalent will be different, depending on which we follow.)*

5) Menaion Feasts during the Paschal Cycle

Finally, it is helpful to add some of the special feasts from the Menaion to the pages for Triodion and Pentecostarion, by way of reminder *(see p.82, or HD p.90-91)*.

TABLE OF CONTENTS

OVERVIEW OF THE PASCHAL CYCLE

Saturday evening, in Vespers: Beginning of the Triodion
♦ **Sunday of the Publican & Pharisee**
♦ **Sunday of the Prodigal Son**
♦ **Sunday of the Last Judgment**
Cheesefare Week
♦ **FORGIVENESS SUNDAY** *(Eve of Great Lent)*
First Week of Great Lent
♦ **1st Sunday: The Triumph of Orthodoxy**
Second Week
♦ **2nd Sunday: St Gregory Palamas**
Third Week
♦ **3rd Sunday: Veneration of the Life-giving Cross**
Fourth Week
♦ **4th Sunday: St John Climacus**
Fifth Week: Great Canon & Feast of the Akathist
♦ **5th Sunday: St Mary of Egypt**
Sixth Week – on Friday: End of the 40 Days
♦ **LAZARUS SATURDAY**
♦ **PALM SUNDAY**
The Great and Holy Week
♦ **PASCHA   + CHRIST IS RISEN ! +**
The Bright Week of Renewal
♦ **THOMAS SUNDAY**
♦ **Sunday: The Holy Myrrhbearers**
♦ **Sunday: The Paralytic**
WED: MID-PENTECOST
♦ **Sunday: The Samaritan Woman**
♦ **Sunday: The Blind-born Man**
WED: LEAVETAKING OF PASCHA
THU: ASCENSION
♦ **Sunday of the Holy Fathers**
♦ **PENTECOST**
MONDAY OF THE HOLY SPIRIT
♦ **Sunday of All Saints** – *End of the Pentecostarion*

THE DATE OF PASCHA &
WEEKDAYS FOR ANY GIVEN DATE

In order to find the weekday for any given date, every date in the calendar is marked with one of seven letters (A-G, counting backwards). *For any given year, <u>from the First of March onwards, until the end of next February</u>, all dates with equivalent letters will fall on the same weekday.* The table below gives the weekday for the beginning of the Church Year (A = 1/14 Sep OC, *or* 1 Sep NC) and the letter-equivalent for all related Sundays (from previous March 1st until the end of next Feb). *Years in a grey band are leap-years. An asterisk (*) marks when the Western Easter date will be the same.* [NB: The weeks in Jan-Feb match the letter-equivalent for the previous year AD. For example, for Jan-Feb 2025, see the details for Pascha/Sep AD 2024.]

Year AD	Date of Pascha (OC = civil)	OC: A = 1/14 Sep	Sun. on:	NC: A = 1 Sep	Sun. on:
2000	17 Apr = 30/4	A = Thu	E	A = Fri	F
2001	2 Apr = 15/4*	Fri	F	Sat	G
2002	22 Apr = 5/5	Sat	G	Sun	A
2003	14 Apr = 27/4	Sun	A	Mon	B
2004	29 Mar = 11/4*	Tue	C	Wed	D
2005	18 Apr = 1/5	Wed	D	Thu	E
2006	10 Apr = 23/4	Thu	E	Fri	F
2007	26 Mar = 8/4*	Fri	F	Sat	G
2008	14 Apr = 27/4	Sun	A	Mon	B
2009	6 Apr = 19/4	Mon	B	Tue	C
2010	22 Mar = 4/4*	Tue	C	Wed	D
2011	11 Apr = 24/4*	Wed	D	Thu	E
2012	2 Apr = 15/4	Fri	F	Sat	G

WEEKDAYS FOR AD 2013 – 2036

Year AD	Date of Pascha (OC = civil)	OC: a = 1/14 Sep	Sun. on:	NC: a = 1 Sep	Sun. on:
2013	22 Apr = 5/5	A = Sat	G	A = Sun	A
2014	7 Apr = 20/4*	Sun	A	Mon	B
2015	30 Mar = 12/4	Mon	B	Tue	C
2016	18 Apr = 1/5	Wed	D	Thu	E
2017	3 Apr = 16/4*	Thu	E	Fri	F
2018	26 Mar = 8/4	Fri	F	Sat	G
2019	15 Apr = 28/4	Sat	G	Sun	A
2020	6 Apr = 19/4	Mon	B	Tue	C
2021	19 Apr = 2/5	Tue	C	Wed	D
2022	11 Apr = 24/4	Wed	D	Thu	E
2023	3 Apr = 16/4	Thu	E	Fri	F
2024	22 Apr = 5/5	Sat	G	Sun	A
2025	7 Apr = 20/4*	Sun	A	Mon	B
2026	30 Mar = 12/4	Mon	B	Tue	C
2027	19 Apr = 2/5	Tue	C	Wed	D
2028	3 Apr = 16/4*	Thu	E	Fri	F
2029	26 Mar = 8/4	Fri	F	Sat	G
2030	15 Apr = 28/4	Sat	G	Sun	A
2031	31 Mar = 13/4*	Sun	A	Mon	B
2032	19 Apr = 2/5	Tue	C	Wed	D
2033	11 Apr = 24/4	Wed	D	Thu	E
2034	27 Mar = 9/4*	Thu	E	Fri	F
2035	16 Apr = 29/4	Fri	F	Sat	G
2036	7 Apr = 20/4	Sun	A	Mon	B

WEEKDAYS FOR AD 2037 - 2060

Year AD	Date of Pascha (OC = civil)	OC: a = 1/14 Sep	Sun. on:	NC: a = 1 Sep	Sun. on:
2037	23 Mar = 5/4*	A = Mon	B	A = Tue	C
2038	12 Apr = 25/4*	Tue	C	Wed	D
2039	4 Apr = 17/4	Wed	D	Thu	E
2040	23 Apr = 6/5	Fri	F	Sat	G
2041	8 Apr = 21/4*	Sat	G	Sun	A
2042	31 Mar = 13/4	Sun	A	Mon	B
2043	20 Apr = 3/5	Mon	B	Tue	C
2044	11 Apr = 24/4	Wed	D	Thu	E
2045	27 Mar = 9/4*	Thu	E	Fri	F
2046	16 Apr = 29/4	Fri	F	Sat	G
2047	8 Apr = 21/4	Sat	G	Sun	A
2048	23 Mar = 5/4*	Mon	B	Tue	C
2049	12 Apr = 25/4	Tue	C	Wed	D
2050	4 Apr = 17/4	Wed	D	Thu	E
2051	24 Apr = 7/5	Thu	E	Fri	F
2052	8 Apr = 21/4*	Sat	G	Sun	A
2053	31 Mar = 13/4	Sun	A	Mon	B
2054	20 Apr = 3/5	Mon	B	Tue	C
2055	5 Apr = 18/4*	Tue	C	Wed	D
2056	27 Mar = 9/4	Thu	E	Fri	F
2057	16 Apr = 29/4	Fri	F	Sat	G
2058	1 Apr = 14/4*	Sat	G	Sun	A
2059	21 Apr = 4/5	Sun	A	Mon	B
2060	12 Apr = 25/4	Tue	C	Wed	D

WEEKDAYS FOR AD 2061 – 2084

Year AD	Date of Pascha (OC = civil)	OC: a = 1/14 Sep	Sun. on:	NC: a = 1 Sep	Sun. on:
2061	28 Mar = 10/4*	**A = Wed**	D	**A = Thu**	E
2062	17 Apr = 30/4	Thu	E	Fri	F
2063	9 Apr = 22/4	Fri	F	Sat	G
2064	31 Mar = 13/4	Sun	A	Mon	B
2065	13 Apr = 26/4	Mon	B	Tue	C
2066	5 Apr = 18/4	Tue	C	Wed	D
2067	28 Mar = 10/4	Wed	D	Thu	E
2068	16 Apr = 29/4	Fri	F	Sat	G
2069	1 Apr = 14/4*	Sat	G	Sun	A
2070	21 Apr = 4/5	Sun	A	Mon	B
2071	6 Apr = 19/4*	Mon	B	Tue	C
2072	28 Mar = 10/4*	Wed	D	Thu	E
2073	17 Apr = 30/4	Thu	E	Fri	F
2074	9 Apr = 22/4	Fri	F	Sat	G
2075	**25 Mar = 7/4***	Sat	G	Sun	A
2076	13 Apr = 26/4	Mon	B	Tue	C
2077	5 Apr = 18/4	Tue	C	Wed	D
2078	25 Apr = 8/5	Wed	D	Thu	E
2079	10 Apr = 23/4*	Thu	E	Fri	F
2080	1 Apr = 14/4	Sat	G	Sun	A
2081	21 Apr = 4/5	Sun	A	Mon	B
2082	6 Apr = 19/4*	Mon	B	Tue	C
2083	29 Mar = 11/4	Tue	C	Wed	D
2084	17 Apr = 30/4	Thu	E	Fri	F

WEEKDAYS FOR AD 2085 - 2099

Year AD	Date of Pascha (OC = civil)	OC: a = 1/14 Sep	Sun. on:	NC: a = 1 Sep	Sun. on:
2085	2 Apr = 15/4*	A = Fri	F	A = Sat	G
2086	25 Mar = 7/4	Sat	G	Sun	A
2087	14 Apr = 27/4	Sun	A	Mon	B
2088	5 Apr = 18/4	Tue	C	Wed	D
2089	18 Apr = 1/5	Wed	D	Thu	E
2090	10 Apr = 23/4	Thu	E	Fri	F
2091	26 Mar = 8/4*	Fri	F	Sat	G
2092	14 Apr = 27/4	Sun	A	Mon	B
2093	6 Apr = 19/4	Mon	B	Tue	C
2094	29 Mar = 11/4	Tue	C	Wed	D
2095	11 Apr = 24/4*	Wed	D	Thu	E
2096	2 Apr = 15/4*	Fri	F	Sat	G
2097	22 Apr = 5/5	Sat	G	Sun	A
2098	14 Apr = 27/4	Sun	A	Mon	B
2099	30 Mar = 12/4*	Mon	B	Tue	C

Letter-equivalents relative to the Sunday

Sun	Mon	Tue	Wed	Thu	Fri	Sat	1st Sunday in September on OC or NC:
A	G	F	E	D	C	B	1/14 or 1
G	F	E	D	C	B	A	2/15 or 2
F	E	D	C	B	A	G	3/16 or 3
E	D	C	B	A	G	F	4/17 or 4
D	C	B	A	G	F	E	5/18 or 5
C	B	A	G	F	E	D	6/19 or 6
B	A	G	F	E	D	C	7/20 or 7

A SIMPLE CALCULATION IN CASE OF NEED

The mathematician Carl Friedrich Gauss worked out a simple calculation, based on the ancient rules, to find the Paschal Date for any given year. Due to historical anomalies (in years AD) here given just for AD 1900-etc:

The symbol **R** is used for the remainder, when dividing the year by a certain numerical value (19, 4, 7, 30, and again 7). The symbol **N** designates the year (AD) for which we would wish to calculate the date of Pascha.

To calculate the date of Pascha – which should always fall on a Sunday – we apply the following formulae:

1) Divide the year N by 19. The remainder R we call a:
   R of $(N/19) = a$

2) Divide the year N by 4. The remainder R we call b:
   R of $(N/4) = b$ [if the year is a leap-year, then R=0]

3) Divide the year N by 7. The remainder R we call c:
   R of $(N/7) = c$

The formulae above take into account both the 19-year lunar cycle and the 28-year solar cycle (4x7=28). Those below are related to the months and weekdays:

4) Use the value of a, found above, to calculate value d:
   R of $[(19a+15)/30] = d$

5) Use values b, c and d, found above, to calculate e:
   R of $[(2b+4c+6d+6)/7] = e$

6) To find the date of Pascha, we now calculate the variable $f = d+e+22$.

The constant 22 is derived from the requirement that Pascha should fall after the vernal equinox (after the ancient Jewish Passover, of which it is the fulfillment).

7) The value of *f* – calculated above – gives us a total number of days from the beginning of March, *including* March 1 (so March 1 plus *f=30* is not 31 Mar but 30 Mar). ***This is the date for the Sunday of Pascha according to the ancient Church Calendar*** *(Julian/Old Style: OC).* To find the current civil date (Gregorian Calendar) we have to add the difference between these calendars:

♦ For AD 1900-2099 we add 13 days for the civil date.
♦ In AD 2100 the difference increases to 14 days, since this is a regular leap-year in the Julian calendar, but not in the Gregorian calendar (because that skips certain leap-years) – so for that century, to find the Gregorian date we would have to add 14 days.

AN EXAMPLE FOR AD 2024:

N = 2024
a = R of (2024/19) = 10
b = R of (2024/4) = 0 [so this is a leap-year]
c = R of (2024/7) = 1

d = R of [(19x10 + 15)/30] = 25
e = R of [(2x0 + 4x1 + 6x25 + 6)/7] = 6
f = 25 + 6 + 22 = 53

So Pascha AD 2024 was on 53 March
→ minus 31 = OC 22 April
→ plus 13 days = 5 May, on the civil calendar.

One 20th-century explanation of this calculation added the following note: 'We would advise the reader to preserve these formulae for the frightful day of the coming age of the Antichrist. Having determined the day of Pascha, we can also easily determine the relationship between movable and immovable Feasts, and thus construct the Church Calendar for a particular year for ourselves.' +

FASTING & DISPENSATION

The traditional Orthodox Christian attitude is basically ascetic, striving to curb our earthly passions for the sake of the true life in Christ. Fasting is one of the tools in this struggle – not intended to destroy the body, but aiming for *the royal path* that enables us to live prayerfully: neither weighed down by rich foods, nor exhausted from efforts beyond our strength. The following levels of fasting and dispensation are the common and time-tested practice of the Church *(for details see HD, p.28-ff)*.

Prayer and Fasting:

(x)   Strict Fast *(or else, xerophagia)*
(r)   Regular Fast-day

Feasts on a Fast-day:

(w)   Wine only *(no oil)*
(o)   Oil
   (SO) - Sa/Su: oil
   (Mo) - Mo: oil
(fs)   Fish

Periods without fasting:

(d)   Diary (inc. eggs)
(FF)   Fast-free

General Practice

♦ Regular Fast: on Wed & Fri, unless otherwise noted (in the monastic setting usually also on Monday).
♦ No regular or strict fasting on Sat/Sun, using at least oil – except for Holy Saturday (then wine only).
♦ Dispensation of fish for the feast of the main church of the local community (monastery, parish, diocese).
♦ Dispensation of oil on any Monday when we celebrate a saint whose relics are present – also during the Nativity Fast and Apostle Fast (not in Great Lent, nor during the Dormition Fast).
♦ Special dispensation for a saint/feast (general or local practice) as noted in the calendar used by the house/community.

Four Fasting Periods

♦ *Great Lent & Dormition Fast:*
Regular fast, except on Sat/Sun (oil). [*Great Lent: Some fast more strictly in the 1st Week, 4th Week, and/or Holy Week (esp. after the Twelve Gospels) – then normally also spending those days in prayer & church services.*]

♦ *Apostle Fast:*
Regular fast, except Tue/Thu (oil) & Sat/Sun (fish).

♦ *Nativity Fast – also known as Christmas Lent:*
Regular fast, except on Tue/Thu & Sat/Sun (oil). In addition, an ancient tradition allows fish on Sat/Sun from the Feast of the Entry of the Theotokos (21 Nov/4 Dec) to the Feast of St Spyridon (12/25 Dec) inclusive. Christmas Eve is generally kept as a fast-day (SO). [As noted in *HD (p.31, Fish)* some local traditions allow fish more often, esp. for greater celebrations – in one old rule until 10/23 Dec (no fish after that, and no oil on weekdays after 20 Dec). But local calendar details do vary.]

Fasts of a Single Day

Regular Fast on any weekday, but on Sat/Sun oil:
♦ Christmas Eve, 24 Dec (6/1).
♦ Eve of Theophany, 5 Jan (18/1).
♦ Feast of the Cross, 14 Sep (27/9).
♦ Beheading St John the Baptist, 29 Aug (11/9).

Fast-free Weeks

All foods permitted to man, also on Wed/Fri:
♦ First week of the Triodion, from the Sunday of the Publican & Pharisee.
♦ Bright Week, from the Sunday of Pascha.
♦ Last week of the Pentecostarion, from Pentecost to the Sunday of All Saints.
♦ During 'the Twelve Days' of Christmas, except for the Eve of Theophany, i.e.: 25 Dec - 4 Jan (7-18/1).
♦ *Dairy only:* In the week before Great Lent, dairy & eggs allowed every day, also Wed/Fri (but no meat).

HONOURING THE FEASTS

When preparing for a Baptism, Wedding, or Memorial Service, it is wise (as well as a matter of basic courtesy) to communicate, *first of all,* with the Priest, *i.e. before setting a definite date or arranging anything else for the occasion.* Thus we shall be able to celebrate properly, according to local usage, as well as making sure that the Priest will be available.

No weddings on the following days (subject to local usage): Exaltation of the Cross (14/27 Sep). Nativity Fast & Christmas/ Nativity (in some areas not until Theophany). Theophany (inc. the Eve). From Sunday of the Last Judgment to Pascha, inc. both days (in some areas also not in Bright Week). Apostle Fast (some allow exceptions). Dormition Fast. Beheading of St John the Baptist (29 Aug/9 Sep). Not on Wed/Fri *[NB: Some forbid the eve of Wed/Fri instead]* – but in some areas allowed when meat is permitted (inc.1st week Triodion & after Pentecost). Strictly speaking, not on any Great/Major Feasts or Patronal Feast (inc. the Eve), nor on the Eve of Sundays – but some make allowances on certain feasts (and/or Sat).

Memorial Services (Trisagion, Panichida) are common on: Memorial Saturdays & most Saturdays (often after the Liturgy, rather than on Sunday). Immediately after someone's *repose,* as well as during the first *forty days* – especially on the *3rd, 9th, and 40th day (the day of repose counts as day one);* then again after three, six, and nine months; and then yearly on (or near) the date of repose. *Immediately after repose, memorials and burial services will, of course, be served. But regular memorial services are usually not served on the following days:* From Lazarus Saturday till Thomas Sunday inclusive. The Patronal Feast of the church. Elevation of the Cross (14/21 Sep). Great/Major Feasts of the Lord and the Theotokos, i.e. Christmas, Circumcision ICXC, Theophany, Meeting ICXC, Annunciation, [Palm Sunday & Pascha, *as included above*], Ascension, Pentecost, Transfiguration, Dormition, Birth of the Theotokos, Entry of the Theotokos into the Temple. +

THE LITURGICAL YEAR

MENAION & PASCHAL CYCLE

The yearly calendar is based on the ancient Menaion date, common to all. For celebrating according to the traditional Julian Calendar (OC/Old Style) the current civil date has been added in brackets – e.g. the liturgical year begins on **1 Sep (14/9)**. Another common way to note this, is by giving double dates, like this: **1/14 Sep**. [NB: For saints of the 20th century there may be different Menaion dates OC/NC, with the same civil date.]

JULY ~ AUGUST

SPECIAL CELEBRATIONS

1/14 July Sts Cosmas & Damian, of Rome.
2 (15/7)   Hon. Garment of the Theotokos.
              NC: St John of Shanghai & San Francisco.
4 (17/7)   OC: Royal Martyrs.
5 (18/7)   OC: NwM Elizabeth & Barbara.
10 (23/7) Vn Anthony of the Kiev Caves.
15 (28/7) EqAp Vladimir of Kiev.
17 July   NC: Royal Martyrs.
18 July   NC: NwM Elizabeth & Barbara.
19 (1/8)   Vn Seraphim of Sarov, relics.
20 (2/8)   Prophet Elijah [Elias].

Practical note: The yearly Menaion begins in September. For convenience, this calendar section includes a few pages for the preceding weeks (as well as at the end, for Sep-Dec). The Paschal cycle has been inserted in the Menaion – so at the start of the Triodion, in Jan/Feb, one can easily skip forward to those pages *(see notes on p.82 and/or HD p.90-91)*. After the Pentecostarion, we continue the Menaion, in May/June *(p.131-ff)*.

22 (4/8)	EqAp Mary Magdalen.
25 (7/8)	Dormition St Anna.
27 (9/8)	GtM Panteleimon, Unmerc. Physician.
31 (13/8)	Forefeast of the Cross.
1/14 August – *Beginning of the Dormition Fast:*	Procession of the Life-giving Cross
5 (18/8)	Forefeast.
6 (19/8)	♦ **Transfiguration.**
13 (26/8)	Leavetaking.
14 (27/8)	Forefeast.
15 (28/8)	♦ **Dormition of the Theotokos.**
16 (29/8)	Afterfeast & Holy Mandylion. >>> *p.t.o.*

✤ AUGUST /September

16 Aug **AFTERFEAST. Holy Mandylion.**
(29/8) Mrt Diomedes. *Prince-Mrt*
  Oil *Constantine Brâncoveanu (RO).*

C

17 Aug Mrt Myron of Cyzicus.
(30/8) *Mrt Straton & comp.*

B

18 Aug Mrt Florus & Laurus.
(31/8) *Vn Arsenius the New, of Paros.*

A

19 Aug GtM Andrew Stratelates
(1/9) & 2,593 soldiers with him.

G

20 Aug Prophet Samuel. *Mrt Reginus*
(2/9) *& Orestes (CY).*

F

Daily commemorations: The structure of the services allows for a combination of two celebrations (feast/saint or group of saints). Calendar entries in this workbook concentrate on the most common dedications (see *HD* for more saints and additional details).

No prayer, my children, gets lost.

+ *Elder Iakovos (Tsalikis)*

---

21 Aug   **Ap(70) Thaddaeus (c.44)**.
  (3/9)   *Vn Martha (Maria) of Diveyevo.*
  Oil

E

22 Aug   Martyr Agathonicus & comp.
  (4/9)   [*Tr:* Mrt Lupus]. *NC: Archpr
             Alexis of Ugine.*

D

23 Aug   **LEAVETAKING**. [Mrt Lupus.
  (5/9)   *HrM Irenaeus, Bp of Lyons*].
  Mo:oil

C

✠ AUGUST /September

24 Aug (6/9) HrM Eutyches. *EqAp Cosmas Aitolos. St Peter of Moscow (SLV). OC: NwM priest Maxim Sandovich.*

B

25 Aug (7/9) Ap(12) Bartholomew (relics). Ap(70) Titus, Bp of Gortyna.

A

26 Aug (8/9) *Oil* **Icon Vladimirskaya (1395, SLV).** Mrt Adrian & Natalia. *Vn Joasaph, son of King Abenner.*

G

27 Aug (9/9) Vn Poemen [Pimen] the Great. *GtM Phanurius of Rhodes.*

F

28 Aug (10/9) [*Some:* ***Leavetk (Mo)***]. Vn Moses the Black. *Vn Job of Pochaev. NC: Repose Elder Joseph the Hesychast.*

E

Sunday 31 Aug - 6 Sep (13-19/9): Sts Peter & Febronia of Murom (relics, SLV), with special prayers for the family – *see note on p.147.*

There is no work on earth that is holier, higher, more magnificent, more significant, more life-giving, than the Divine Liturgy.

+ St John of Kronstadt

29 Aug	**BEHEADING OF**
(11/9)	**ST JOHN THE BAPTIST**
Fast/	
SO	

D

30 Aug	**AFTERFEAST** [*one day*]. Sts
(12/9)	Alexander, John & Paul the New,
	of C'ple. *St Alexander Nevsky (SLV).*

C

31 Aug	**Girdle [Sash] of the Theotokos.**
(13/9)	*Vn Eanswyth, Abbess. St Aiden*
Oil	*of Lindisfarne.*

B

✠ SEPTEMBER

1 Sep   **CHURCH NEW YEAR (INDICT).**
(14/9)   **Vn Simeon Stylites.**
Oil

A

2 Sep   Martyr Mamas. Vn John the
(15/9)   Faster, Patr of C'ple.

G

3 Sep   HrM Anthimus. Vn Theoctistus,
(16/9)   fellow-ascetic of Vn Euthymius.

F

4 Sep   HrM Babylas of Antioch. Proph
(17/9)   Moses, 'who beheld God'.

E

*If you desire eternal health,
listen to your conscience,
do all it tells you,
and you will benefit.*

+ *St Mark the Ascetic*

5 Sep	Prophet Zachariah & Elizabeth,
(18/9)	parents of St John the Forerunner.

D

6 Sep	**Miracle of the Archangel**
(19/9)	**Michael at Colossae/Chonae.**
Oil	

C

7 Sep	**FOREFEAST.** Martyr Sozon
(20/9)	of Cilicia.

B

✠ SEPTEMBER

8 Sep   + **NATIVITY OF THE MOST-**
(21/9) **HOLY THEOTOKOS** +
Fish

A

---

9 Sep   **Synaxis Rgt Joachim & Anna.**
(22/9) Mrt Severian. *3rd Oec.Council.*
  Oil

G

---

10 Sep   Martyrs Menodora, Metrodora
(23/9) and Nymphodora, at Nicomedia.

F

---

11 Sep **OC: Vn Silouan the Athonite.** Vn
(24/9) Theodora. [*Tr:* HrM Autonomus]
OC:oil

E

---

12 Sep **LEAVETAKING.**
(25/9) [HrM Autonomous, Bp in Italy]
Mo:oil

D

Put off the old man in order to lead a
new life, bridling in thyself everything
that leads unto death ... and let us only
remember the old so that we may avoid it.
Thus man is consecrated, and thus we
will honour this day of the Consecration.

+ *Menaion 13 Sep. Vespers of the*
Dedication (Consecration).

13 Sep   **FOREFEAST. Dedication: Church**
(26/9)   **of the Resurrection, Jerusalem.**
Mo:oil   HrM Cornelius. *GtM Ketevan (GE).*

C

14 Sep   **+ EXALTATION OF THE LIFE-GIVING**
(27/9)   **CROSS** + *6th Oec. Council (EL).*
Fast
(SO)

B

15 Sep   GtM Nicetas the Goth. *St Joseph*
(28/9)   *the New of Partoş (RO).*

A

✚ SEPTEMBER /October

16 Sep **GtM Euphemia the All-**
(29/9) **praised, of Chalcedon.**
  Oil

G

17 Sep Martyrs Sophia & her daughters
(30/9) Faith, Hope and Love (at Rome).

F

18 Sep Vn Eumenius the Wonderworker,
(1/10) Bp of Gortyna on Crete.

E

19 Sep Martyrs Trophimus, Sabbatius &
(2/10) Dorymedon, of Synnada.

D

20 Sep GtM Eustathius, his wife
(3/10) Theopiste & their two sons.

C

> True love in the heart is like a pure fire or
> warmth that sets a person aglow; it is the
> root which produces in him all good work.
>
> *+ St Innocent of Alaska*

21 Sep   **LEAVETAKING**. [Ap Quadratus]
(4/10)   *St Demetrius of Rostov (relics: SLV).*

B

22 Sep   HrM Phocas. [*Tr:* Ap Quadratus]
(5/10)   *HrM Theodosius of Brazi (RO).*

A

23 Sep   Conception of St John, Fore-
(6/10)   runner and Baptist of the Lord.
Oil

G

✤ SEPTEMBER /October

24 Sep **NC: Vn Silouan the Athonite.**
(7/10) ProtoM & EqAp Thecla.
NC:oil

F

25 Sep **Vn Sergius of Radonezh (SLV).**
(8/10) Vn Euphrosyne.
Oil

E

26 Sep **ApEv John the Theologian.**
(9/10) *St Neagoe Basarab (RO).*
Oil

D

27 Sep Mrt Callistratus. *Vn Sabbatius of*
(10/10) *Solovki (SLV). HrM Anthimus (RO).*

C

28 Sep **Vn Neophytus the Recluse (KY:**
(11/10) **relics).** Vn Chariton of Palestine.
Oil

B

> While we look not at the things which are
> seen, but at the things which are not seen:
> for the things which are seen are temporal;
> but the things which are not seen
> are eternal.
>
> *+ 2Cor.4:18, KJV*

29 Sep	Vn Cyriacus the Hermit. *OC: St*
(12/10)	*John of Shanghai & San Fr (relics).*

A

30 Sep	HrM Gregory of Armenia.
(13/10)	*St Michael of Kiev (SLV).*

G

✝ OCTOBER

1 Oct   **POKROV: Holy Protection**. Ap(70)
(14/10)   Ananias. Vn Romanus the Melodist.
Oil

F

2 Oct   HrM Cyprian & VirginM Justina
(15/10)   of Nicomedia.

E

3 Oct   HrM Dionysius the Areopagite
(16/10)   & comp. *Patron Saints, Korea.*

D

4 Oct   St Hierotheus, Bp of Athens.
(17/10)

C

He who desires that which God wishes,
has the Angels as his guides.
He who bears slander with humility,
has reached perfection
and the Angels marvel at him.

+ St Isaac the Syrian

5 Oct   Martyr Charitina (304). *Holy*
(18/10) *Hierarchs of Moscow (SLV).*

B

6 Oct   Ap(12) Thomas Didymus.
(19/10)
   Oil

A

7 Oct   Martyrs Sergius & Bacchus. *OC:*
(20/10) *St Jonah of Hankov, Manchuria.*

G

✠ OCTOBER

8 Oct   Vn Pelagia the Penitent, on the
(21/10) Mount of Olives.

F

9 Oct   Ap(12) James, son of Alphaeus.
(22/10) Vn Andronicus & Athanasia.
Oil

E

10 Oct   Vn Ambrose of Optina (SLV)
(23/10) [*some: Synaxis Vn Startsi of Optina*]
Oil   Mrt. Eulampius & Eulampia.

D

11 Oct   Ap & Dcn Philip. St Theophanes the
(24/10) Branded. [*some: Synaxis Vn Startsi
         of Optina*].

C

12 Oct   *SLV:* St Martin the Merciful.
(25/10) Mrt Probus & comp. *SLV/RO:* Vn
SLV:oil Cosmas, Hymnogr.

B

Celebration of the 7th Oecumenical Council:
Always celebrated on Sunday, on or after 11/24
Oct (i.e. Sunday 11/24 - 17/30 Oct). But some
traditions celebrate this on the nearest Sunday:
between 8/21 - 14/27 Oct.

*Watch ye, stand fast in the Faith,
quit you like men, be strong.*

- 1Cor.16:13

13 Oct   Martyrs Carpus & comp. *Transl.*
(26/10) *relics of Ap Andrew to Iaşi (RO).*

A

14 Oct   Vn Parasceva (Petka) of Thrace
(27/10) *(BU,SE,RO).* Mrt Nazarius & comp.
  Oil   *EL:* Vn Cosmas, Hymnogr.

G

15 Oct   Vn Martyr Lucian of Antioch.
(28/10)

F

✤ OCTOBER /November

16 Oct   Martyr Longinus the Centurion,
(29/10)   who stood at the Cross of the Lord.

E

17 Oct   Prophet Hosea (820 BC). Vn
(30/10)   Mrt Andrew of Crete, at Crisis.

D

18 Oct   **ApEv Luke**. *GtM Zlata [or:*
(31/10) *Chryse], repose (BU).*
  Oil

C

19 Oct   Prophet Joel. *Martyr Varus.*
(1/11)   *Vn Frideswide. Vn John of Rila.*

B

20 Oct   GtM Artemius. *Vn Gerasimus*
(2/11)   *the New (EL). OC: Vn Gabriel*
          (Urgebadze) of Samtavro (GE).

A

Memorial Saturday before St Demetrius: On the Saturday between 19-25 Oct (1-7/11), in some churches, *Demetrius' Saturday of Ancestors*, with special Commemoration of the Departed.

'Every good thing that is given, and every perfect gift, is from above ...

+ James 1:17

21 Oct	Vn Hilarion the Great. *NwM &*
(3/11)	*Conf Bessarion & comp (RO).*

G

22 Oct	EqAp Abercius. The Seven Youths
(4/11)	of Ephesus. *Kazan Icon (SLV).*

F

23 Oct	**Ap(70) James, brother of the**
(5/11)	**Lord & First Bp of Jerusalem.**
Oil	

E

✤ OCTOBER /November

24 Oct   GtM Arethas. *Icon of the Theotokos*
(6/11)   *'Joy of All Who Sorrow'.*

D

25 Oct   Martyrs Marcian & Martyrius
(7/11)   the Notaries.

C

26 Oct   GtM Demetrius, the Myrrh-
(8/11)   flowing. *Great Earthquake, C'ple.*
Oil

B

27 Oct   Martyr Nestor. *Vn Demetrius the*
(9/11)   *New (relics in Bucharest: RO).*

A

28 Oct   Martyrs Terence, Neonilla & their
(10/11) 7 children. *Vn Job of Pochaev.*

G

On October 28th (10/11) also: GtM Parasceva of Iconium (SLV). Vn Diomedes (CY). Vn John the Chozebite (SLV). HrM Neophit (GE). Vn Stephen the Sabbaite. St Arsenius I, of Peć (SE). St Athanasius I, Patr of C'ple. St Iachint of Wallachia (RO). St Demetrius of Rostov (SLV). Panagia Eleutherotria (EL). *OC also :* Vn Arsenius of Cappadocia (1924). *NC also:* St Athanasius, Bp of Kostrov (1962).

Be ye holy, for I am holy.

+ *1Peter 1:16*

29 Oct (11/11)	VgM Anastasia the Roman. Vn Abramius the Recluse & St Mary.

F

30 Oct (12/11)	HrM Zenobius & Mrt Zenobia. *Sts Stefan Milutin, Dragutin & Elena of Serbia (SE).*

E

31 Oct (13/11)	Ap(70): Stachys, Aristobulus & others. Mrt Epimachus.

D

✠ NOVEMBER

1 Nov **Wonderw Unmerc Cosmas &**
(14/11) **Damian, Mesopotamia (Asia).**
Mo:oil

C

2 Nov Mrt Acyndinus. *NC: Vn Gabriel*
(15/11) *(Urgebadze) of Samtavro (GE).*

B

3 Nov **GtM George (relics, KY). Mrt**
(16/11) Acepsimas, Joseph & Aithalas.
Oil

A

4 Nov St Joannicius the Great. HrM
(17/11) Nicander of Myra & Hermas.

G

Remember that after temptation comes spiritual joy,
and that the Lord protects them that
endure temptations and suffering
for the sake of His love.

+ *St Nectarius of Ægina*

5 Nov	Martyrs Galaction & Episteme.
(18/11)	*Ap(70) Linus (EL/CY). St Jonah of Novgorod (SLV).*

F

6 Nov	HrM Paul of C'ple. *Vn Barlaam*
(19/11)	*[Varlaam] of Khútyn (SLV).*

E

7 Nov	The 33 Martyrs of Melitene.
(20/11)	*St Willibrord. OC: Priest George Calciu (RO).*

D

✛ NOVEMBER

8 Nov **Synaxis: Archangel Michael**
(21/11) **& Bodiless Powers of Heaven**.
Oil

C

9 Nov **St Nectarius of Aegina.** Mrt One-
(22/11) siphorus & Porphyrius. Vn Matrona.
Oil *OC: Vn Elder Iakovos (Tsalikis).*

B

10 Nov   Ap(70) Olympas, Herodian, Sosi-
(23/11)   pater & others. Martyr Orestes.

A

11 Nov   GtM Menas, Mrt Victor, Vincent
(24/11)   & Stephanida. Vn Theodore, Studite.

G

12 Nov *EL:* **St John the Merciful**
(25/11) **& St Martin the Merciful.**
EL:oil

F

On 15/28 Nov we begin the **Nativity Fast** – for details on dispensation during this period, see p.17.

Continue in prayer, and watch in the same with thanksgiving.

+ *Colossians 4:2*

13 Nov	**St John Chrysostom, Archbp**
(26/11)	**of C'ple**.
Oil	

E

14 Nov	**Ap Philip, of the Twelve**.
(27/11)	*St Gregory Palamas.*
Oil	

D

15 Nov	BEGINNING OF THE NATIVITY FAST.
(28/11)	Mrt Gurias, Samonas & Abibus.
	Vn Païsius Velichkovsky.

C

✚ NOVEMBER /December

16 Nov **ApEv Matthew**. *St Sergius*
(29/11) *of Malopinega, priest.*
  Oil

B

---

17 Nov   Vn Gregory the Wonderw, Bp of
(30/11) Neocaesarea. *Vn Hilda of Whitby.*

A

---

18 Nov   GtM Plato of Ancyra. Mrt Dcn
 (1/12) Romanus & youth Barulas.

G

---

19 Nov   Proph Obadiah. Mrt Barlaam, at
 (2/12) Antioch. *St Philaret of Moscow*
         (SLV). OC: Vn Elder Porphyrius.

F

---

20 Nov   **FOREFEAST**. Vn Gregory of
 (3/12) Decapolis. St Proclus of C'ple.
         NC: Pr George Calciu (RO).

E

From **the Feast of the Entry** onwards, we begin to chant the *Katavasia* of the Nativity (Matins).

> *Be still
> and know that I am God.*

+ Psalm 45/46

21 Nov
(4/12) + **ENTRY OF THE THEOTOKOS INTO THE TEMPLE** +

Fish

D

22 Nov   Ap(70) Philemon, Archippus &
(5/12)   Mrt Apphia. Mrt Cecilia & comp.
          NC: Vn Elder Iakovos (Tsalikis).

C

23 Nov   St Amphilochius. St Gregory of
(6/12)   Agrigentum. *St Alexander Nevsky.*
          Vn Anthony of Iezerul-Vâlcea (RO).

B

✤ NOVEMBER /December

24 Nov   *SLV:* **GtM Catherine of Alx'a.**
(7/12)   *EL:* HrM Clement & Peter.
SLV:oil

A

25 Nov   **LEAVETAKING** *[KY on 26th].*
(8/12)   *EL/KY:* **GtM Catherine of Alx'a.**
Mo:oil   *SLV:* HrM Clement & Peter.
EL:oil

G

26 Nov   *[KY, Transf:* **LEAVETAKING.**] Vn
(9/12)   Alypius, Stylite. *Vn Stylianos (CY/EL).*
KY:Mo   *St Innokenty of Irkutsk (SLV).*

F

27 Nov   GtM James the Persian. *SLV:* Vn
(10/12)   Palladius of Thess. *Kursk-root*
          Icon 'Of the Sign'.

E

28 Nov   Vn Martyr Stephen the New of
(11/12)   Mt St Auxentius. Mrt Irenarchus.

D

> Man is a great mystery, a sacred mystery of God. So great and so sacred, that God Himself became man, in order to explain to us all the depth of the mystery of man.
>
> *+ St Justin Popovitch*

29 Nov (12/12)   Mrt Paramon & comp. *SLV:* Vn Acacius (from THE LADDER).

C

30 Nov (13/12)   **Ap Andrew, the First-called.**

Oil

B

✤ DECEMBER

1 Dec   Prophet Nahum. *Vn Philaret the*
(14/12) *Merciful, in Paphlagonia.*

A

2 Dec   Prophet Habakkuk [Avvacum].
(15/12) *NC: Vn Elder Porphyrius.*

G

3 Dec   Prophet Zephania [Sophonias].
(16/12) *Vn Sabbas [Savva] of Zvenigorod.*

F

4 Dec   GtM Barbara & Mrt Juliana.
(17/12) Vn John Damascene.
   Oil

E

Rejoice, O Isaiah! The Virgin has conceived in her womb, and borne a Son, Emmanuel, both God and man. Orient is His name; and, magnifying Him, we call the Virgin blessed.

+ Matins 1 Dec. Irmos 9th Ode

5 Dec **Vn Sabbas the Sanctified**.
(18/12)
Oil

D

6 Dec **St Nicholas the Wonderworker,**
(19/12) **Archbp of Myra in Lycia**.
Oil

C

7 Dec   St Ambrose, Bp of Milan.
(20/12) *EL: Martyrs of Africa. Mrt*
Philothea the New (relics, RO).

B

✦ DECEMBER

8 Dec   FOREFEAST of the Conception by
(21/12) St Anna. Vn Patapius of Thebes.
         SLV: Martyrs of Africa..

A
***
9 Dec   **Conception by Rgt Anna of the**
(22/12) **Theotokos**. *Icon 'Unexpected Joy'.*
Oil

G
***
10 Dec   Mrt Menas, Hermogenes &
(23/12)   Eugraphus, at Alx'a. *Mother
          Angelina of Albania/Serbia (SE).*

F
***
11 Dec   Vn Daniel the Stylite of C'ple.
(24/12)

E
***
12 Dec   **St Spyridon the Wonderw**. [*Some*
(25/12)   *today: Vn Herman & Am. Martyrs.*]
Oil

D
***

Sunday of the Holy Forefathers: On 11/24 - 17/30 Dec – preparing for the Feast of the Nativity.

By faith didst Thou justify the forefathers, O Thou Who, through them, didst betroth Thyself aforetime to the Church from among the nations. The saints boast in glory, for from their seed has come a right glorious fruit, even she who gave Thee birth....

+ Doxasticon, Vespers for the Forefathers

13 Dec **[Vn Herman of Alaska,** *HrM*
(26/12) *Juvenaly & Mrt Peter the Aleut.*] Mrt
Oil Eustratius. VgM Lucy [*or on 14th*]

C

14 Dec   Mrt Thyrsus, Leucius & Callinicus.
(27/12)   Mrt Philemon & comp, at Alx'a.

B

15 Dec **HrM Eleutherios**. *St Stephen of*
(28/12) *Sourozh. OC: New HrM Hilarion*
Oil *(Troitskii).*

A

✦ DECEMBER /January

16 Dec Prophet Haggai [Aggaeus]. *St*
(29/12) *Theophano. St Modestus II (EL).*

G

17 Dec **Proph Daniel & the 3 Youths:**
(30/12) **Ananias, Azarias & Misael.**
Oil

F

18 Dec **St Modestus I, Patr of Jer. (KY).**
(31/12) *Vn Daniel of Sihastria (RO).*
Mo:oil

E

19 Dec Martyr Boniface of Tarsus in
(1/1) Silicia

D

20 Dec **FOREFEAST. HrM Ignatius of**
(2/1) **Antioch. St John of Kronstadt.**
Oil

C

Sunday before the Nativity: On 18-24 Dec (31/12-6/1), celebrating the Genealogy & all the Righteous from Adam to Rgt Joseph the Betrothed.

For our God, Whom we serve, is able to deliver us from the burning fiery furnace, and he will rescue us from thy hand, O king. But if not, be it clear unto thee, O king, that we will not serve thy gods, nor worship the golden image which thou hast set up.

+ Daniel 3:17-18

21 Dec   VgM Juliana of Nicomedia
  (3/1)   & comp.

B

22 Dec   GtM Anastasia (Pharmacolytria).
  (4/1)   *OC: Vn Nicephorus the Leper.*

A

23 Dec   Ten Holy Martyrs of Crete.
  (5/1)   *St Nahum of Ochrid.*

G

✛ DECEMBER /January

24 Dec **EVE OF THE NATIVITY.** Nun-
(6/1) Mrt Eugenia of Rome & comp.
Fast
(SO)

F

25 Dec **+ NATIVITY IN THE FLESH**
(7/1) **OF OUR LORD ICXC +**
Pascha
& FF

E

26 Dec **Synaxis of the Theotokos**.
(8/1) St Euthymius, Bp of Sardis.
Pascha
& FF

D

27 Dec **Third Day of the Feast.** Proto-
(9/1) martyr & Archdcn Stephen.
Pascha
& FF

C

28 Dec The 20,000 Martyrs at Nicomedia
(10/1) *NC: New HrM Hilarion (Troitskii).*
Fast-
free

B

Sunday after the Nativity: On Sunday 26-31 Dec (8-13/1) or, if no Sunday, on the 26th, celebrating Rgt Joseph the Betrothed, Prophet-King David and St James, Brother of the Lord.

Heaven and earth are united today, for Christ is born!

+ Nativity, Lity

29 Dec (11/1) *Fast-free*	The Infants slain at Bethlehem. *[Remembering all Christians who died a cruel death for the True Faith]*

A

30 Dec (12/1) *Fast-free*	VgM Anysia. [*Tr:* Vn Melania of Rome]. *Ap(70) Timon.*

G

31 Dec (13/1) *Fast-free*	**LEAVETAKING.** [St Melania (the Younger) of Rome].

F

✠ JANUARY

---

1 Jan   **CIRCUMCISION OF OUR LORD**
(14/1)   **ICXC. St Basil the Great.**
Fast-
free

E

---

2 Jan   **FOREFEAST. St Seraphim of**
(15/1)   **Sarov**. St Sylvester of Rome.
Fast-
free

D

---

3 Jan   Proph Malachi. Mrt Gordius.
(16/1)   *Virgin Genevieve of Paris.*
Fast-
free

C

---

4 Jan   **Synaxis of the Seventy Apostles**.
(17/1)   Vn Theoctistus of Cuocomo.
Fast-   *NC: Vn Nicephorus the Leper.*
free

B

__Saturday/Sunday after Theophany:__ Between 7/20-13/26 Jan, with special readings for the Liturgy.

At Theophany, the Great Blessing of the Waters is done on the Eve of the Feast (usually in church) and again on the day itself, after the Liturgy – then often outdoors.

Walk in newness of life.

+ Romans 6:4

5 Jan	**EVE OF THEOPHANY**. HrM Theo-
(18/1)	pemptus & Theonas. Vn Syncletica.
Fast	
(SO)	

A

6 Jan	**+ THEOPHANY +**
(19/1)	
Fast-	
free	

G

7 Jan	**Synaxis of St John, Prophet,**
(20/1)	**Forerunner & Baptist**.
Fish	

F

✢ JANUARY

8 Jan   Vn George the Chozebite. Vn
(21/1) Domnica. *Mrt Isidore, parish-
        priest of Yuryev & comp.*

E

9 Jan   Martyr Polyeuctus of Melitene in
(22/1) Armenia. St Philip of Moscow.

D

10 Jan Sts Gregory of Nyssa & Theosevia.
(23/1) St Marcian, priest. *St Theophan
        the Recluse (SLV).*

C

11 Jan   Vn Theodosius the Great, the
(24/1)   Cenobiarch.
Oil

B

12 Jan Mrt Tatiana of Rome. *St Theodora
(25/1) of Alx'a. [SLV, Tr: St Sava of Serbia]*

A

The First Sunday of the Triodion can fall from OC 11 Jan (24/1) to OC 14 Feb (27/2) – n leap years from OC 12 Jan (25/1) to OC 15 Feb (28/2).

Let the study of Holy Scripture and the Fathers be your food and rest, and your pleasure be prayer and divine Communion.

+ *Elder Amphilochius Makris*

13 Jan (26/1)	Mrt Hermylus & Stratonicus. *[Transf: Vn Frs of Sinai & Raithu. EL: St Sava. SE: Leavetaking]*

G

14 Jan (27/1) *Oil*	**LEAVETAKING**. EqAp Nina. *[Vn Fathers of Sinai & Raithu. SE: St Sava [Sabbas] I, Archbp of Serbia.]*

F

15 Jan (28/1)	Vn Paul of Thebes. Vn John the Kalyvite ('hut-dweller').

E

✤ JANUARY /February

16 Jan   Veneration of the Chains of Ap
(29/1)   Peter. *Mrt Speusippus & comp.*

D
_____

17 Jan   Vn Anthony the Great.
(30/1)
   Oil

C
_____

18 Jan   St Athanasius the Great &
(31/1)   St Cyril [Kirill] of Alx'a.
   Oil

B
_____

19 Jan   St Mark (Eugenikos) of Ephesus.
(1/2)   Vn Macarius the Great, Egypt.
   Oil   *Vn Macarius of Alexandria.*

A
_____

20 Jan   Vn Euthymius the Great.
(2/2)
   Oil

G
_____

Sunday nearest 25 Jan (OC): (i.e. 22-28 Jan /
4-10 Feb) Synaxis of All the New Martyrs &
Confessors under the Atheist Yoke (SLV).

*And when these things begin to come to
pass, then look up, and lift up your heads,
for your redemption is drawing nigh.*

+ Luke 21:28

21 Jan	Vn Maximus the Confessor. Mrt
(3/2)	Neophytus of Nicaea. *Vn Maximus the Greek.*

F

22 Jan	Ap(70) Timothy. Monk-Mrt
(4/2)	Anastasius the Persian.

E

23 Jan	HrM Clement of Ancyra & Mrt
(5/2)	Agathangelus. *[6th Oec. Council – some on 14/27 Sep]*

D

✤ JANUARY /February

24 Jan **Blessed Xenia of St Petersb** (SLV).
(6/2) *Vn Xenia of Rome. Vn Neophytus*
Oil *the Recluse (sign/miracle, CY).*

C

---

25 Jan **St Gregory the Theologian**. *New*
(7/2) *HrM Vladimir, Metr of Kiev (SLV).*
Oil

B

---

26 Jan   Vn Xenophon & Mary. *Vn Theodore*
(8/2)   *the Studite (relics). St David II (the*
Restorer), King of Georgia (GE).

A

---

27 Jan **Translation of the relics of St**
(9/2) **John Chrysostom (to C'ple).**
Oil

G

---

28 Jan   Vn Ephraim the Syrian.
(10/2)   *Vn Isaac the Syrian.*

F

Beginning of the Triodion: On both CC/NC, all the faithful begin the Triodion together; but there is a difference relative to the Menaion. <u>On the civil calendar</u> the Triodion begins between 24/1-27/2 *(for the OC equivalent, see p.61)* .

Humblemindedness and the fear of God are above all virtues.

+ Abba John Kolovos

29 Jan (11/2)	HrM Ignatius the God-bearer, of Antioch (relics). 7 Martyrs of Samosata. *Vn Gildas the Wise.*

E

30 Jan **(12/2)** Oil	**SYNAXIS OF THE THREE HIERARCHS.** *Blessed Pelagia of Diveyevo, Fool-for-Christ.*

D

31 Jan (13/2)	Mrt Unmerc Cyrus & John, with Martyrs Athanasia & daughters.

C

✠ FEBRUARY

---

1 Feb   **FOREFEAST. Mrt Tryphon. Vn**
(14/2)   **Brigid of Kildare**.
   Oil

B

---

2 Feb   **+ MEETING OF THE LORD: at**
(15/2)   **the Presentation in the Temple +**
  Fish

A

---

  3 Feb   *Before Lent:* **AFTERFEAST**.
(16/2)   Synaxis Rgt Simeon & Anna.
      EqAp Nicholas of Japan.

G

---

  4 Feb   Vn Isidore of Pelusium.
(17/2)

F

St Tryphon: In some regions, after the Divine Liturgy, procession around the village to bless the fields, vineyards, gardens and orchards (with Holy Water from Theophany, or doing the Lesser Blessing of Water) – in some places with special prayers for protection of the cultivated land & crops, and that in all this ...

"... the most-holy Name be glorified, of the Father, and of the Son, and of the Holy Spirit."

5 Feb	Martyr Agatha of Palermo. *St*
(18/2)	*Theodosius of Chernigov (SLV).*

E

6 Feb	St Bucolus of Smyrna.
(19/2)	*Vn Barsanuphius & John.*
	St Photius the Great.

D

7 Feb	St Parthenius, Bp of Lampsacus.
(20/2)	*NC: New HrM Vladimir, Kiev (SLV).*

C

✠ FEBRUARY

8 Feb *Before Lent:* **GtM Theodore**
(21/2) **Stratelates ('the General').**
[Mo]

B

9 Feb *Before Lent:* **LEAVETAKING.**
(22/2) *OC: Uncovering of relics of St*
[Mo] *Tikhon of Moscow (SLV).*

A

10 Feb *Before Lent:* **HrM Charalampus**
(23/2) **[Haralambos]**. *St Scholastica.*
[Oil]

G

11 Feb HrM Blasius of Sebaste. *St Theo-*
(24/2) *dora the Empress (who restored*
veneration of the Holy Icons).

F

12 Feb St Meletius of Antioch. *St Alexis,*
(25/2) *Metr of Kiev & Moscow (SLV).*
NwM Christos the Gardener (CY).

E

Some saints are only celebrated **before Lent**, as noted [if their feast day falls during Lent, there is no special dispensation].

Rejoice in the Lord, alway,
and again I say, Rejoice.

+ *Philippians 4:4*

| 13 Feb | Vn Martinian, Sts Zoe & Photini |
| (26/2) | [*or:* Svetlana]. |

D

| 14 Feb | Vn Auxentius, monk of Bithynia. |
| (27/2) | *OC: St Raphael, Bp of Brooklyn.* |

C

| 15 Feb | Ap(70) Onesimus. |
| (28/2) | |

B

✤ FEBRUARY /March

16 Feb   Martyr Pamphylius. *EL: St*
 (1/3)   *Flavian, Patr of C'ple.*
L: 29/2

A

---

17 Feb   *Before Lent:* **GtM Theodore**
 (2/3)   **Tyron ('the Recruit').** *Empress*
L: 1/3   *Pulcheria. OC: St Nicholas Planas.*
 [Oil]

G

---

18 Feb   St Leo the Great, Pope of Rome.
 (3/3)   *SLV: St Flavian, Patr of C'ple.*
L: 2/3

F

---

19 Feb   Ap(70) Archippus & comp. *Vn*
 (4/3)   *Dositheus, disciple of Abba*
L: 3/3   *Dorotheus.*

E

---

20 Feb   St Leo the Wonderworker, Bp
 (5/3)   of Catania.
L: 4/3

D

> *We find ourselves on the ocean of life;
> sometimes we will have storms, and
> sometimes calm. God does not forsake us.
> Otherwise, if He did not keep us, we
> would have drowned already.*
>
> *+ Elder Amphilochius Makris*

21 Feb   Vn Timothy of Symbóla. *St
(6/3)   Eustathius [Eustace] of Antioch.*
L: 5/3

C

22 Feb   Uncovering Relics of Martyrs at
(7/3)   the Gate of Eugenius (C'ple).
L: 6/3   *Vn Thalassius & Limnaeus.*

B

23 Feb   HrM Polycarp, Bp of Smyrna.
(8/3)   *Uncovering Relics of Bl. Matrona
L: 7/3   of Moscow (SLV).*

A

✠ FEBRUARY /March

24 Feb **1st & 2nd Finding of the**
(9/3) **Head of St John the Baptist.**
L: 8/3 *[disp. see p.82]*
[Disp]

G

25 Feb St Tarasius, Patr of C'ple.
(10/3)
L: 9/3

F

26 Feb St Porphyrius, Archbp of Gaza.
(11/3)
L: 10/3

E

27 Feb Vn Procopius the Decapolite.
(12/3) *NC: St Raphael, Bp of Brooklyn.*
L: 11/3

D

28 Feb Vn Basil, fellow-ascetic of Vn
(13/3) Procopius the Decapolite.
L: 12/3

C

When it is not a leap-year, **Vn John Cassian** and other saints named on 29 February, may be celebrated/commemorated on the 28th instead.

Casting all your care upon Him,
for He cares for you.

+ *1 Peter 5:7*

NB: February 28/29th is the end of the **sequence of weekdays** related to the previous Year/Pascha. For the Sundays and other weekdays from March 1st onwards, we need to use the letter-equivalent for the coming Pascha & Church New Year (see tables and clarification on p.9-13).

29 Feb   Vn John Cassian, the Roman.
L: 13/3

B

✠ MARCH /Apr

C	1 Mar (14/3)	Vn Mrt Eudoxia [Eudocia]. *St David of Wales.*
B	2 Mar (15/3)	Mrt Hesychius. HrM Theodotus. *NC: St Nicholas Planas.*
A	3 Mar (16/3)	Martyrs Eutropius, Cleonicus & Basiliscus.
G	4 Mar (17/3)	Vn Gerasimus, at the Jordan.
F	5 Mar (18/3)	Vn Mrt Conon the Isaurian. *OC: St Nikolai (Velimirovich).*
E	6 Mar (19/3)	The 42 Martyrs of Ammoria.
D	7 Mar (20/3)	Seven HrM's of Cherson.
C	8 Mar (21/3)	Vn Theophylactus, Bp of Nicomedia.
B	**9 Mar (22/3)**	**The 40 Martyrs of Sebaste** *[disp, p.82].*
A	10 Mar (23/3)	Mrt Quadratus [Codradus] of Corinth & comp.
G	11 Mar (24/3)	St Sophronius, Patr of Jerusalem.
F	12 Mar (25/3)	Vn Theophanes the Confessor. St Gregory, Dialogist.
E	13 Mar (26/3)	St Nicephorus, Patr of C'ple (relics).
D	14 Mar (27/3)	Vn Benedict of Nursia
C	15 Mar (28/3)	Mrt Agapius & comp.

When reading the Holy Scriptures, he who is humble and engaged in spiritual work will apply everything to himself and not to someone else.

+ *Vn Mark the Ascetic*

B	16 Mar (29/3)	Mrt Sabinus [Sabinas]. *Vn Christodoulos of Patmos.*
A	17 Mar (30/3)	Vn Alexis, the Man of God. *Vn Patrick, Ireland,*
G	18 Mar (31/3)	St Cyril of Jerusalem. *NC: Nikolai (Velimirovich).*
F	19 Mar (1/4)	Martyrs Chrysanthos & Daria.
E	20 Mar (2/4)	Vn Frs slain at St Sabbas' Monastery. *Vn Cuthbert.*
D	21 Mar (3/4)	Vn James the Confessor. *OC: Vn Seraphim of Vrytsa.*
C	22 Mar (4/4)	HrM Basil of Ancyra
B	23 Mar (5/4)	Vn Martyr Nikon, Bp & disciples.
A	24 Mar (6/4)	**FOREFEAST**. Vn Artemon. [*Tr:* St Tikhon of Moscow]
G	**25 Mar** **(7/4)**	**+ ANNUNCIATION** *[disp, p.82]* *OC: St Tikhon of Moscow, Vn Justin (Popovich).*
F	26 Mar (8/4)	Synaxis Archangel Gabriel [*celebration depends on Lent*].
E	27 Mar (9/4)	Mrt Matrona of Thessalonica.
D	28 Mar (10/4)	Vn Hilarion the New. Vn Stephen the Wonderw.
C	29 Mar (11/4)	St Mark of Arethusa & comp (under Julian the Apostate).
B	30 Mar (12/4)	Vn John (Climacus) of Sinai.
A	31 Mar (13/4)	HrM Hypatius. EqAp Innocent of Moscow/Alaska.

✤ MARCH /April

✢ APRIL /May

G	1 Apr (14/4)	Vn Mary of Egypt.
F	2 Apr (15/4)	Vn Titus the Wonderw, of the Studion Monastery.
E	3 Apr (16/4)	Vn Nicetas the Confessor. *NC: Vn Seraphim of Vrytsa.*
D	4 Apr (17/4)	Vn George, Mt Maleon [*some:* & Vn Joseph, Hymnogr]
C	5 Apr (18/4)	*EL:* Mrt Claudius. *SLV:* Mrt Agathopodes & Theodulus.
B	6 Apr (19/4)	St Eutychius of C'ple.
A	7 Apr (20/4)	Mrt Calliopus. St George of Mytilene. *NC: St Tikhon of Moscow, Vn Justin (Popovich).*
G	8 Apr (21/4)	Ap(70) Herodion, Agabus, Rufus & others.
F	9 Apr (22/4)	Mrt Eupsychius of Caesarea in Cappadocia.
E	10 Apr (23/4)	Mrt Terence & comp, at Carthage.
D	11 Apr (24/4)	HrM Antipas of Pergamum. *St Callinicus of Cernica (RO).*
C	12 Apr (25/4)	Vn Basil of Parium. *Mrt Sabbas the Goth (RO).*
B	13 Apr (26/4)	*EL:* St Martin, Pope of Rome. *SLV:* Mrt Artemon,
A	14 Apr (27/4)	*EL:* Ap(70) Aristarchus, Pudens & Trophimus *SLV:* St Martin, Pope of Rome.
G	15 Apr (28/4)	*SLV:* Ap(70) Aristarchus, Pudens & Trophimus. *EL:* Martyr Crescens.

Do not fight to expel the darkness from
the chamber of your soul.
Open a tiny aperture for light to enter,
and the darkness will disappear.

+ Elder Porphyrius of Kavsokalyvia

F	16 Apr (29/4)	VgM Agape, Irene & Chionia.
E	17 Apr (30/4)	HrM Simeon of Persia & comp. Vn Acacius, Melitene.
D	18 Apr (1/5)	Vn John the Isaurian.
C	19 Apr (2/5)	HrM Paphnutius. Vn John of the Ancient Caves. *OC: Bl. Matrona of Moscow.*
B	20 Apr (3/5)	Vn Theodore Trichinas (with the 'Hairshirt').
A	21 Apr (4/5)	HrM Januarius & comp. HrM Theodore of Perge.
G	22 Apr (5/5)	Vn Theodore the Sykeote.
F	**23 Apr (6/5)**	**GtM George (*after Lent*, o).**
E	24 Apr (7/5)	Vn Elizabeth, Wonderw. Mrt Sabbas Stratelates. *HrM Joseph, Elias & others (RO).*
D	**25 Apr (8/5)**	**ApEv Mark (*after Lent*, o).** *Vn Basil [Vasile] (RO).* *OC: Repose Elder Philotheos (Zervakos).*
C	26 Apr (9/5)	HrM Basil of Amasea. *St Stephen, Bp of Perm (SLV).*
B	27 Apr (10/5)	Ap(70) & HrM Simeon, kinsman of the Lord.
A	28 Apr (11/5)	*EL:* 9 Martyrs of Cyzicus. *SLV:* Ap(70) Jason & Sosipater.
G	29 Apr (12/5)	*EL:* Ap(70) Jason & Sosipater. *SLV:* 9 Mrt of Cyzicus.
F	**30 Apr (13/5)**	**Ap James of Zebedee (o).** *St Ignatius Brianchaninov.*

✢ APRIL /May

FEASTS OF THE MENAION DVRING THE PASCHAL CYCLE

The Triodion starts somewhere between *Sun 11/24 Jan - 14/27 Feb (L: 12/25 Jan - 15/28 Feb)*, depending on the date of Pascha. From that day onwards, the celebration of the Menaion takes second place, but a few feasts are always celebrated:

In February:

♦ **2 Feb (15/2): THE MEETING OF THE LORD**
   (fish) – also the 1st week of Lent (but the Afterfeast is not celebrated in Lent: instead, cut short or omitted).

♦ **24 Feb (9/3, L: 8/3): First & Second Finding of the Head of the Forerunner, St John the Baptist**
   (disp) – dispensation of oil, except in the first week of Lent (but then there will be a cooked meal after the Presanctified and some special consolation of fasting food without oil etc. – KY: halva, tahini, olives)

In March:

♦ **9 Mar (22/3): The Forty Martyrs of Sebaste**
   (disp) – as for St John the Baptist, see above.

♦ **25 Mar (7/4): THE ANNUNCIATION**
   (disp) – The Feast often falls in Great Lent, but there is dispensation of fish on any day, except for Great Fri-Sat (wine only). The Feast is always chanted in full, even combined with the Paschal Vigil (i.e. at *Kyriopascha*).

♦ **[26 Mar (8/4), Synaxis of the Archangel Gabriel:** Celebration depends on when it falls. Some allow oil also on this day, but <u>not</u> in 1st Week, nor in Holy Week.]

*When the following feast days fall in Great Lent or Holy Week, they may be **transferred** to Bright Week (after Mon):*

♦ **23 Apr (6/5): GtM George (o)**
♦ **25 Apr (8/5): ApEv Mark (o)**

*For further **celebrations during the Pentecostarion**, see the Menaion pages (Mar-Apr: p.76-ff, May-June: p.131-ff).*

THE PASCHAL CYCLE

Open unto me, O Giver of Life, the gates of repentance: for early in the morning my spirit seeks Thy holy temple ...

(Triodion, Matins 1st Sunday)

SATURDAY – *Eve of the Triodion* –

Commonly celebrated:
♦ Vespers/Vigil for Sunday: Beginning of the Triodion

✠ SUNDAY
of the Publican and the Pharisee

First Sunday of the Triodion
Commonly celebrated:
♦ Divine Liturgy

MON First Week of the Triodion (FF)
– All week Fast-free, also Wed/Fri –

TUE

WED

Preparations: From now on, in Sunday Matins, we chant the set of Lenten hymns that begin, "Open unto me..." On the next three Sundays we will ponder on our exile from the true life in God, chanting the lament of the Babylonian exile (Ps.136/137).

Let us humble ourselves before God,
and with fasting cry aloud as the Publican:
God be merciful to us sinners.

~ Triodion, Vespers 1st Sunday

THU

FRI

SAT

Commonly celebrated:
♦ [Divine Liturgy & Memorials]
♦ Vespers/Vigil for Sunday

✠ SUNDAY
of the Prodigal Son

Second Sunday of the Triodion

Commonly celebrated:
♦ Divine Liturgy

MON Second Week of the Triodion
– Last week of Meatfare –

TUE

WED

Last week of Meatfare: This Thursday, in certain areas, friends will share a last festive meal with meat – the Sunday being spent with the family: a homely way to prepare together for Great Lent.

> *... at least from this day, from this hour,*
> *from this moment, [let us] strive*
> *to love God above all else,*
> *and to fulfull his holy will.*
>
> + *St Herman of Alaska*

THU

[*Local practice:* Festive meal]

FRI

MEMORIAL SATURDAY

Commonly celebrated:
♦ Divine Liturgy & Memorial Service
♦ Vespers/Vigil for Sunday

✚ SUNDAY
of the Last Judgment

Third Sunday: Last day of Meatfare
Commonly celebrated:
♦ Divine Liturgy

MON Cheesefare Week (d)
    – Dairy & eggs, also on Wed/Fri –

TUE

---

*In the church services for Wednesday, from
Vespers onwards:* PRAYER OF ST EPHRAIM.

WED

Until the 9th Hour: PRAYER OF ST EPHRAIM.

Last week of Cheesefare: In many areas, pancakes (local style). Wed/Fri fast-free, but church services are Lenten in character.

The springtime of the Fast has dawned, the flower of repentance has begun to open. O brethren, let us cleanse ourselves from all impurity and sing to the Giver of Light: Glory be to Thee, Who alone lovest mankind.

+ *Triodion, Cheesefare Week:*
Vespers for Wed

THV

In the church services for Friday, from
Vespers onwards: PRAYER OF ST EPHRAIM.

FRI

Until the 9th Hour: PRAYER OF ST EPHRAIM.

SAT   Commemoration of the Holy Ascetics

Commonly celebrated:
♦ [Divine Liturgy & Memorials]
♦ Vespers/Vigil for Sunday

✚ FORGIVENESS SUNDAY

Remembering the Expulsion of Adam from Paradise (d)

This last Sunday before Lent
is the last day of Cheesefare.
Tomorrow we begin the Great Fast.

Commonly celebrated:
♦ Divine Liturgy
♦ **Vespers of Forgiveness**

PURE MONDAY - First Week of Great Lent

Commonly celebrated:
♦ **Great Canon (1)**

TUE

Commonly celebrated:
♦ **Great Canon (2)**

WED

Commonly celebrated:
♦ Vespers & Presanctified
♦ **Great Canon (3)**

The three most comprehensive virtues of the soul are prayer, silence and fasting. Thus you should refresh yourselves with contemplation of created realities when you relax from prayer; with conversation about the life of virtue when you relax from silence; and with such food as it permitted when you relax from fasting.

+ Elias the Presbyter (Philokalia)

THU

Commonly celebrated:
♦ **Great Canon (4)**

FRI

Commonly celebrated:
♦ Vespers & Presanctified [**Kolyva for St Theodore**]
♦ [*local:* Small Compline with Akathist (1)]

SAT   St Theodore the Recruit

Commonly celebrated:
♦ [Divine Liturgy & Memorials]
♦ Vespers/Vigil for Sunday

✚ SUNDAY

The Triumph of Orthodoxy

First Sunday in Lent

Commonly celebrated:
♦ Divine Liturgy (of St Basil the Great)
& Procession with the Holy Icons
♦ Lenten Vespers

MON *Second Week of Lent*

TUE

WED

Commonly celebrated:
♦ Vespers & Presanctified

With all our strength, let us remain faithful
and unshaken in all that we have received
from the divine Apostles, and the
Holy Fathers and Teachers of the Church.

+ Elder Philotheos (Zervakos)

THU

FRI

Commonly celebrated:
♦ Vespers & Presanctified
♦ [*local:* Small Compline with Akathist (2)]

SAT

Commonly celebrated:
♦ [Divine Liturgy & Memorials]
♦ Vespers/Vigil for Sunday

✚ SUNDAY
of St Gregory Palamas

Second Sunday in Lent
Commonly celebrated:
♦ Divine Liturgy (of St Basil the Great)
♦ Lenten Vespers

MON *Third Week of Lent*

TUE

WED

Commonly celebrated:
♦ Vespers & Presanctified

The true aim of the Christian life consists in the acquisition of the Holy Spirit. Fasting, prayer, and all good works, done in the name of Christ, are but a means to that end. And the best way is to concentrate on those things which bring us most profit ....

+ St Seraphim of Sarov

THU

FRI

Commonly celebrated:
♦ Vespers & Presanctified
♦ [*local:* Small Compline with Akathist (3)]

SAT

Commonly celebrated:
♦ [Divine Liturgy & Memorials]
♦ Vespers/Vigil for Sunday – *In the Vigil (end of Matins)* **the Cross is brought out** *after the Great Doxology.*

✚ SUNDAY

Veneration of the Life-Giving Cross

Third Sunday in Lent

Commonly celebrated:
- ♦ Divine Liturgy (of St Basil the Great)
- ♦ Lenten Vespers

MON Fourth Week of Lent

TUE

WED

Commonly celebrated:
- ♦ Vespers & Presanctified

The Week of the Cross marks the middle of Great Lent.

> ### Before thy Cross we bown down, O Master, and thy holy Resurrection we glorify.
>
> *+ at the veneration*
> *of the Cross*

THV

FRI

Commonly celebrated:
- Vespers & Presanctified – *During this service, at the end of the Typika,* **the Cross is carried back into the Altar.**
- [*local:* Small Compline with Akathist (4)]

SAT

Commonly celebrated:
- [Divine Liturgy & Memorials]
- Vespers/Vigil for Sunday

✚ SUNDAY
of St John Climacus

Fourth Sunday in Lent

Commonly celebrated:
♦ Divine Liturgy (of St Basil the Great)
♦ Lenten Vespers

MON Fifth Week of Lent

TUE

WED *Special dispensation:* (o)

Commonly celebrated:
♦ **Vespers (with the 24 Penitential Stichera) & Presanctified**
♦ **Service of the Great Canon** – *In some traditions this service
 also includes the reading of the Life of Vn Mary of Egypt.*

My soul, O my soul, wake up,
why art thou sleeping? ...

+ *Kontakion of the*
Great Canon

Fifth Week (cont.)

THU   + OF THE GREAT CANON +
Special dispensation: **(o)**

Commonly celebrated:
♦ Vespers & Presanctified *(as consolation
  after the efforts of the Great Canon)*

FRI   *Special dispensation:* **(w)**

Commonly celebrated:
♦ Vespers & Presanctified
♦ **Festive Service of the Akathist** – *this may simply be done
  in the evening, or as part of a Night-time Vigil (inc. Liturgy)*

SAT   + OF THE AKATHIST +

Commonly celebrated:
♦ [*Divine Liturgy*] – *in some places part of the Vigil last night*
♦ Vespers/Vigil for Sunday

We all sing in honour of thy Son, O Theotokos,
            and praise thee as a living temple.
For the Lord who holds all things in His hand
            made His dwelling in thy womb ...

Rejoice, O Bride unwedded!

+ Akathist, Ikos 12/23

✠ SUNDAY
of St Mary of Egypt

Fifth Sunday in Lent

Commonly celebrated:
- ◆ Divine Liturgy (of St Basil the Great)
- ◆ Lenten Vespers

MON Sixth Week of Lent

TUE

WED

Commonly celebrated:
- ◆ Vespers & Presanctified

As we begin with eagerness, O ye faithful, the sixth week of the holy Fast, let us sing a hymn in preparation for the Feast of Palms, to the Lord who comes with glory to Jerusalem in the power of the Godhead, that He may slay death ...

+ 5th Sunday, Vespers on Sunday Evening

> Wednesday Matins (sessional hymns):
Today dead Lazarus is buried, and his sisters sing in lamentation ...
"Lazarus sleeps," Thou hast prophesied to Thy disciples, "but I go to raise up him whom I created."

Sixth Week (cont.)

THU

FRI **– Completing the Forty Days –**

Commonly celebrated:
♦ **Vespers for Lazarus Saturday**
  & Presanctified

+ LAZARVS SATVRDAY +

Commonly celebrated:
♦ **Divine Liturgy of the Feast**
♦ **Vespers/Vigil for Palm Sunday** – *Traditionally, where the Vigil is celebrated, at the end of Matins the Blessing of Palms.*

Having completed the forty days that bring profit to our soul, we beseech Thee ... Grant us also to behold the Holy Week of thy Passion ...

+ *Vespers for Lazarus Saturday*

✚ PALM SUNDAY
The Entry into Jerusalem

(dispensation for the feast: **fish**)

Commonly celebrated:
♦ **Divine Liturgy** – *Some do the Matins in the morning, with the Blessing of Palms shortly before the Liturgy.*
♦ **Vespers** – *entering Holy Week.*
♦ **Bridegroom Matins (1)**

MON – Joseph the Virtuous –

Commonly celebrated:
♦ Vespers & Presanctified
♦ **Bridegroom Matins (2)**

TUE – The Ten Virgins –

Commonly celebrated:
♦ Vespers & Presanctified
♦ **Bridegroom Matins (3)**

WED – XC Anointed with Myrrh –

Commonly celebrated:
♦ Vespers & Presanctified *(Prayer of St Ephraim: last time)*
♦ **Holy Unction** *(for all the faithful – done in most places)*
♦ **Matins of the Washing of the Feet**

A traditional practice in this week is the **continuous reading of all four Gospels**. Some communities do this in the services (Mon-Wed), some arrange time for doing so privately, each by himself. Following an ancient tradition, such continuous reading may also be done during the prayerful watch in church, in the night from Fri-Sat (after the Liturgy continuing with Acts).

> **I see thy bridal chamber adorned, O my Saviour, and I have no wedding garment that I may enter there. Make the robe of my soul to shine, O Giver of Light, and save me.**
>
> *+ Exapostilarion for Holy Week*

Great and Holy Week (cont.)

THU – The Mystical Supper –

Commonly celebrated:
♦ **Vespers & Liturgy of St Basil** – *special dispensation after the Liturgy* (o), *but after the Twelve Gospels strict fast.*
♦ **Matins of the Twelve Gospels** *(the Cross is brought out)*

FRI – The Lord's Saving Passion –

Commonly celebrated:
♦ **Royal Hours**
♦ **Vespers** – *the Epitaphion is brought out.*
♦ **Matins with Lamentations** *(Burial Procession)*

After Vespers and/or Matins: prayerful watch in church (see note on p.107)

SAT – The Descent into Hades –

Commonly celebrated:
♦ **Vespers (OT Readings) & Liturgy of St Basil** – *special disp. after the Liturgy* (w) *[in some places also: nuts & dried fruit].*
♦ *Easter Night:* **The Paschal Night-Vigil**

The **Paschal Night-Vigil** begins with a short Midnight Office, during which the Epitaphion is carried back into the Altar [*NB: In some places this is done earlier – related to the Saturday Liturgy, or even directly after the Burial procession on Friday evening.*] At the end of the Liturgy: blessing of eggs and other traditional paschal fare; in some communities also the Blessing of the Artos.

> ### ... but like the Thief will I confess Thee:
> ### Remember me, O Lord,
> ### when Thou comest into thy kingdom.

*+ Apolytk.on for
Holy Thursday*

✢ HOLY PASCHA

& the Bright Week of Renewal

IͨC XͨC
NI KA

[*Most places will have celebrated Liturgy
in the Paschal Night-Vigil.*]
*From now on, no kneeling – also not
privately – until the Kneeling Prayers at
Pentecost. Bright Week is entirely fast-free.*

Commonly celebrated:
✦ **Paschal Vespers** *(known as 'Agape')*

MON   *Today, after the Liturgy, in some places a festive
procession all around the village or neighbourhood.*

Commonly celebrated:
✦ **Paschal Liturgy**
✦ **Paschal Vespers for Bright Tuesday**

TVE   *Special celebrations (local), including:*
Icon 'Axion Estin'. Martyrs Raphael, Nicholas & Irene.

Commonly celebrated:
✦ **Paschal Liturgy**
✦

WED

[*In some places, every day of Bright Week the
Paschal Liturgy, with Vespers on the Eve.*]
✦
✦

✠ Christ is Risen ✠

Bright Week of Renewal (cont.)

THU

Commonly celebrated:
- ♦
- ♦ Paschal Vespers for Bright Friday

FRI   + THE LIFE-GIVING SPRING +

Commonly celebrated:
- ♦ **Paschal Liturgy** *(afterwards, in some places:*
  the Lesser Blessing of Water)
- ♦ **Paschal Vespers for Bright Saturday**

SAT

Commonly celebrated:
- ♦ **Paschal Liturgy** *(in some places also:*
  the prayer for the cutting/breaking of the Artos)
- ♦ **Vespers/Vigil for Thomas Sunday**

+ ΧΡΙΣΤΌΣ ΑΝΈΣΤΙ + ΧΡЇСТÓСЬ ВОСКРÉСЕ + HRISTOS
A ÎNVIAT + ATGYFODODD CRIST + LE CHRIST EST
RESUSCITÉ + CHRIST IST ERSTANDEN + CHRISTUS IS
OPGESTAAN + CHRIST IS RISEN +

... HE IS RISEN INDEED !

✠ THOMAS SUNDAY
(the Eighth Day of Pascha)

Second Sunday of Pascha
Commonly celebrated:
♦ Divine Liturgy

MON *Second week after Pascha*

TUE

Today, in some traditions:
♦ **Joyous Commemoration of
the Departed** ('Radonitsa')

WED

During the Pentecostarion some traditions do not fast strictly on Wed/Fri (using at least oil). Others (inc. KY) resume the usual ascetic fast on Wed/Fri after Bright Week (though for those who keep the Monday fast, *Mo:oil*).

> *This is the day which the Lord has made:*
> *let us rejoice and be glad in it.*
>
> *+ Ps.117/118*

THU

FRI

SAT

Commonly celebrated:
♦ [Divine Liturgy & Memorials]
♦ Vespers/Vigil for Sunday

✠ SUNDAY
of the Holy Myrrhbearers

Third Sunday of Pascha
Commonly celebrated:
♦ Divine Liturgy

MON Third week after Pascha

TUE

WED

Ye Myrrhbearing women,
why do you come to the tomb?
why do you seek the Living among the dead?
Take courage, the Lord is risen!

+ Sunday Holy Myrrhbearers, Lity

THU

FRI

SAT

Commonly celebrated:
♦ [Divine Liturgy & Memorials]
♦ Vespers/Vigil for Sunday

✠ SUNDAY
of the Paralytic

Fourth Sunday of Pascha
Commonly celebrated:
♦ Divine Liturgy

MON *Fourth week after Pascha*

TUE

Commonly celebrated (insofar possible):
♦ **Vespers/Vigil for Mid-Pentecost**

WED ✠ MID-PENTECOST ✠
Disp.: **fish**.

Commonly celebrated (insofar possible):
♦ **Divine Liturgy** (*afterwards, in some places, the Lesser Blessing of Water*)

The middle of the days is come, which begin with
the saving Arising of the Lord, and are sealed by
the divine Pentecost. Most solemn are these middle
days, illumined by the radiance of both feasts and
uniting the two, and looking toward the Master's
Ascension: showing forth the glory which is to come.

+ Vespers for Mid-Pentecost

THU

FRI

SAT

Commonly celebrated:
♦ [Divine Liturgy & Memorials]
♦ Vespers/Vigil for Sunday

✛ SUNDAY
of the Samaritan Woman

Fifth Sunday of Pascha
(Sunday of Mid-Pentecost)
Commonly celebrated:
♦ Divine Liturgy

MON *Fifth week after Pascha*

TUE

WED *Leavetaking of Mid-Pentecost*

And she ran to the town, and cried out to the crowd, saying: Come, see the Messiah - the Christ - Who grants to the world the great mercy.

+ *Sunday of the Samaritan*
Woman, in Vespers

THV

FRI

SAT

Commonly celebrated:
♦ [Divine Liturgy & Memorials]
♦ Vespers/Vigil for Sunday

✚ SUNDAY
of the Blind-born Man

Sixth Sunday of Pascha
Commonly celebrated:
♦ Divine Liturgy

MON *Sixth week after Pascha*

TVE

In some places:
♦ **Paschal Vespers.** *And, later in the evening:*
♦ **Night-time Vigil:** Paschal Matins & Liturgy

WED *Leavetaking of Pascha*
Disp.: fish.

♦ [*if no Night-time Vigil, celebration may be
in the morning:* Paschal Matins & Liturgy]
Commonly celebrated:
♦ **Vespers/Vigil for the Feast of the Ascension**

The Day of Resurrection! Let us be radiant, O ye people. Pascha, the Pascha of the Lord, his Passover: For from death to life, and from earth to heaven, Christ our God has made us pass, as we sing a hymn of victory.

+ Paschal Canon, 1s: Irmos

THU + ASCENSION ICXC +

Commonly celebrated:
♦ **Divine Liturgy**

FRI

SAT

Commonly celebrated:
♦ [Divine Liturgy & Memorials]
♦ Vespers/Vigil for Sunday

✤ SUNDAY
of the Holy Fathers

Sunday before Pentecost
Commonly celebrated:
♦ Divine Liturgy

MON *Seventh week after Pascha*

TUE

WED

Thou wast begotten from the Father, without a mother, before the ages and before the morning star. But Arius did not glorify Thee as God - with the senseless daring of his created mind, teaching that Thou art just a creature ... [which would make salvation impossible]. Wherefore the Council at Nicaea proclaimed the truth: that Thou art the Son of God, co-enthroned with the Father and the Holy Spirit.

+ Sunday of the Holy Fathers, in Vespers

THU

FRI *Leavetaking of the Ascension*

MEMORIAL SATURDAY

Commonly celebrated:
♦ Divine Liturgy & Memorial Service
♦ Vespers/Vigil for Pentecost

✙ SUNDAY OF PENTECOST
(Day of the Holy Trinity)

Commonly celebrated:
- **Divine Liturgy**
- **Vespers with the Kneeling Prayers**

MON   + OF THE HOLY SPIRIT +
All week Fast-free, also Wed/Fri.

Commonly celebrated:
- Divine Liturgy

TUE   Third day of the Feast

WED

When the Most High came down
and confused the tongues, He divided he nations,
but when He distributed the tongues of fire,
He called all to unity - therefore with one voice
we glorify the All-Holy Spirit!

+ Kontakion of Pentecost

THU

FRI

SAT *Leavetaking of Pentecost*

Commonly celebrated:
♦ [Divine Liturgy & Memorials]
♦ Vespers/Vigil for Sunday

✤ SUNDAY OF ALL SAINTS
(last day of the Pentecostarion)

First Sunday after Pentecost
Commonly celebrated:
♦ Divine Liturgy

MON Beginning of the Apostle Fast

Dispensation during the Apostle Fast:
Oil on every Tue/Thu, and Fish on Sat/Sun
(when relics also Mo:oil, as noted on p.17)

+ All ye Saints, pray to God for us +

See then that ye walk circumspectly,
not as fools, but as wise:
Redeeming the time,
because the days are evil.

Wherefore be ye not unwise,
but understanding
what is the will of the Lord.

And be not drunk with wine,
wherein is dissipation;
but be filled with the Spirit;

Speaking to yourselves
in psalms and hymns
and spiritual songs,
singing and
making melody in your heart
to the Lord ...

+ Eph. 5:15-19

AFTER ALL SAINTS

CONTINUING THE MENAION

The Sunday of All Saints completes the Pentecostarion, showing forth the first-fruits of Pentecost in the celebration of all those who have already entered into *'the Joy of the Lord'* – inviting us to join that festive procession into the Kingdom. Locally, one or more of the following Sundays may be dedicated to the celebration of an additional Synaxis of Local Saints – celebrating those especially dear to the community.

✠ MAY

1 May   Proph Jeremiah. *St Tamara, Queen*
(14/5)   *of Georgia. St Panaretos (CY).*

E

2 May   **St Athanasius Gt (relics).** *EqAp*
(15/5)   *Michael (BU). Sts Boris & Gleb*
Mo:oil   *(relics). NC: Bl. Matrona of Moscow.*

D

3 **May**   **Vn Theodosius of the Kiev Caves**
(16/5)   **(SLV)**. *Mrt Timothy & Maura.*
Oil

C

4 May   VgM Pelagia of Tarsus. *St Lazarus*
(17/5)   *'of the Four Days' (transl. relics).*

B

Restrain thy thoughts from earthly things,
not only when standing before God in His temple,
but wherever thou art, when obliged
to busy thyself with earthly things ...
lift up thy heart unto heaven and God.

+ *St Philaret of Moscow*

5 May GtM Irene. *Vn NwM Ephraim,*
(18/5) *the Newly Revealed.*

A

6 May Rgt Job. *Vn Job of Pochaev.*
(19/5) *St Seraphim, Mt Dombos (EL).*

G

7 May Sign of the Cross, Jerusalem. Mrt
(20/5) Acacius. *Vn Nilus of Sora. Vn John*
of Zedazneni & Syrian Frs (GE).

F

✠ MAY

8 May **ApEv John the Theologian**.
(21/5) Vn Arsenius the Great. *NC: Elder*
Oil *Philotheos (Zervakos, repose).*

E

9 May Proph Isaiah. *St Nicholas of Myra,*
(22/5) *Wonderw (relics) [EL on 20 May].*

D

10 May Ap(12) Simon Zelotes. *Vn Isidora,*
(23/5) *Fool-for-XC. Blessed Thais.*

C

11 May **EqAp Methodius & Cyril (SLV)**.
(24/5) HrM Mocius.
Oil

B

12 May St Ephiphanius of Cyprus. St
(25/5) Germanus of C'ple. *Mrt John*
the Wallachian (RO).

A

*The quickest and safest path to heaven
is humility. This is the only safe path.*

+ Elder Philotheos (Zervakos)

13 May   VgM Glyceria & Mrt Laodicius,.
(26/5)   *Vn Euthymius [Evfimy], Founder
         of Iveron Monastery (GE).*

G

14 May   Mrt Isidore of Chios. *Vn Serapion
(27/5)   the Sindonite.* HrM Therapon *(CY).
         Blessed Isidore of Rostov.*

F

15 May   St Pachomius the Great.
(28/5)   *St Isaiah, Wonderw of Rostov.*
   Oil

E

✤ MAY /June

16 May   Vn Theodore the Sanctified.
 (29/5)   *Vn Brendan 'the Navigator'.*

D

17 May   Ap(70) Andronicus & Mrt Junia.
 (30/5)   *OC: Vn Jonah Atamanski (1924).*

C

18 May   The 7 Virgin-Martyrs & Martyr
 (31/5)   Theodotus. Mrt Peter & comp.

B

19 May   HrM Patrick [Patricius] of Prusa.
 (1/6)   *13 Vn Monk-Mrt of Kantara (CY).*

A

20 May   Mrt Thalalaeus & comp. *EL: St*
 (2/6)   *Nicholas of Myra [others, 9 May].*

G

> In whatever stage you may be, do not get discouraged. Pray, even if it feels forced, and the Lord will visit you with His mercy ...
>
> *+ Elder Cleopa (Ilie)*

21 May
(3/6)
Oil
Sts Constantine & his mother Helena, Equals-to-the-Apostles.

F

22 May
(4/6)
Mrt Basiliscus of Comana. *Rgt Melchizedek. 2nd Oec Council.*

E

23 May
(5/6)
Vn Michael of Synnada.
Vn Euphrosyne of Polotsk.

D

✠ MAY /June

24 May (6/6)	Vn Simeon of the Wondrous Mountain. *Vn Vincent of Lerins.*

C

25 May   **Third Finding of the Head of**
(7/6)   **the Forerunner**.
Mo:oil

B

26 May   Ap(70) Carpus & Alphaeus.
(8/6)

A

27 May   HrM Therapont of Sardis. EL:
(9/6)   HrM Helladius. *Vn John the*
          Russian (Euboia).

G

28 May   Mrt Eutychius. Mrt Nicetas. *HrM*
(10/6)   *Helladius (SLV). Vn Helena [Elena]*
         of Diveyevo.

F

He is kind to the unthankful and to the evil. Be ye therefore merciful, as your Father also is merciful.

+ *Lk. 6: 35-36*

---

29 May   **OC: St Luke of Simferopol (SLV).**
(11/6)   VgM Theodosia of Tyre. *[Some*
OC: oil   *name also: 1st Oec. Council].*

E

---

30 May   Vn Isaac, Dalmatian Monastery.
(12/6)   *Vn Macrina & Basil, grand-parents*
         of St Basil. NC: Vn Jonah Atamanski.

D

---

31 May   Ap(70) Hermas. Mrt Hermias, at
(13/6)   Comana.

C

✠ JUNE

1 Jun — Mrt Justin the Philosopher.
(14/6) — *OC: Vn Justin (Popovich, SE).*

B

2 Jun — St Nicephorus, Patr of C'ple. *GtM*
(15/6) — *John the New, of Suceava (RO).*

A

3 Jun — Mrt Lucillian, 4 youths & VgM
(16/6) — Paula. *Vn Kevin, Glendalough.*

G

4 Jun — St Metrophanes, C'ple. *Sts Mary &*
(17/6) — *Martha. Mrt Zoticus & comp (RO).*
Vn John of Monagri (CY).

F

All possible care must be taken, that we hold that Faith which has been believed everywhere, always, by all ... This rule we shall observe if we follow universality [the whole Church] - antiquity [the ancient faith of the saints] - consent [agreement in antiquity, by all or at least nearly all].

+ St Vincent of Lerins (24 May/6 Jun)

5 Jun	HrM Dorotheus of Tyre.
(18/6)	*Vn Dorotheus of Gaza. HrM*
	Boniface, Archbp of Mainz.

E

6 Jun	Vn Hilarion the New. *EL: VgM*
(19/6)	*Kyra [Kyriake], Valeria [Caleria]*
	& Marcia [Maria].

D

7 Jun	HrM Theodotus of Ancyra. *SLV:*
(20/6)	*VgM Kyra [Kyriake], Valeria*
	[Caleria], & Marcia [Maria].

C

✦ JUNE

8 Jun   GtM Theodore Stratelates (relics).
(21/6)   *St Ephraim, Patr of Antioch. RO:*
          Mrt Nicander & Marcian.

B

9 Jun   St Cyril of Alx'a. *Vn Columba*
(22/6)   *(Colum Cille) of Iona.*

A

10 Jun   Mrt Alexander & Antonina. HrM
(23/6)   Timothy, Prusa. *Martyrs of China:*
          Metrophan Chi-Sung & comp.

G

11 Jun   Ap Barnabas & Bartholomew.
(24/6)   *NC:* St Luke, Simferopol. Icon
   Oil 'Axion Estin'. *Martyrs of China*

F

12 Jun   Vn Onuphrius the Great. Vn Peter
(25/6)   the Athonite. [*EL: St Triphyllius*].

E

My son, if thou come to serve the Lord,
prepare thy soul for temptation.

+ Sirach 2:1

13 Jun (26/6)	Mrt Aquilina. *SLV/CY/RO:* St Triphyllius, Cyprus. *Vn Alexandra, First Abbess of Diveyevo.*

D

14 Jun (27/6)	Proph Elisha. St Methodius, C'ple. *Synaxis Sts of Diveyevo (SLV). NC: Vn Justin (Popovich).*

C

15 Jun (28/6)	Proph Amos. *Synaxis of All Nw-Mrt of Serbia, from the time of Prince Lazar until the present (SE).*

B

✢ JUNE /July

16 Jun   St Tychon the Wonderw, Cyprus.
(29/6)   *OC: St Theophan the Recluse (SLV).*

A

17 Jun   Mrt Manuel, Sabel & Ishmael.
(30/6)   *EL also: Mrt Isaurus. Vn Mrt*
         Nectan of Hartland.

G

18 Jun   Mrt Leontius & comp, Phoenicia.
(1/7)   *Vn Leontius the Seer, Mt Athos.*

F

19 Jun   Ap(12) Jude, brother of the Lord.
(2/7)   OC: St John of Shanghai [*some*
Oil   *on Sat*]. *Vn Paisius the Great.*

E

20 Jun   HrM Methodius 'of Patara'. *Vn*
(3/7)   *Nahum of Ochrid. Vn Nicholas*
         Cabasilas.

D

Love your enemies: bless them that curse you, do good to them that hate you, and pray for them which despitefully use you, and persecute you.

~ Mt. 5:44

21 Jun Mrt Julian of Tarsus. *Vn*
(4/7)   *Maximus the Greek (SLV).*

C

22 Jun HrM Eusebius of Samosata. *St*
(5/7)   *Gregory [Grigorie] Dascălu (RO).*
        St Alban, ProtoMrt of Britain.

B

23 Jun Mrt Agrippina of Rome & comp.
(6/7)   *Mrt Eustochius, Gaius & comp.*

A

✤ JUNE /July

24 Jun   **NATIVITY OF ST JOHN, Prophet,**
(7/7)   **Forerunner & Baptist**.
Fish

G

25 Jun   **AFTERFEAST** *[one day]*. VgM
(8/7)   Febronia. *Sts Peter & Febronia*
of Murom (SLV).

F

26 Jun   Vn David of Thess. *Vn John*
(9/7)   *of Gothia. Tikhvin Icon (SLV)*.

E

27 Jun   Vn Sampson the Hospitable.
(10/7)   *St Joanna, Myrrhbearer*.

D

28 Jun   Unm's Cyrus & John. *Vn Sergius &*
(11/7)   *Herman. Icon 'Of the Three Hands'*
   OC: Repose Elder Sophrony, Essex.

C

On 25 June (8/7), the Slav tradition also celebrates **Sts Peter & Febronia of Murom** – with special prayers, in and after the Liturgy, for the stability of marriage and family life [*as is <u>also done on the Sunday on or before 6/19 Sep</u>*].

To overcome our own self we do not need to cast it down. What we need to do is to keep it from falling.

+ St Gregory of Nyssa

29 Jun **(12/7)** Fish	**Ap Peter & Paul**. *OC: Repose of Elder Paisius (Ath, 1994).*

B

30 Jun **(13/7)** Oil	**Synaxis of the Twelve Apostles**.

A

✚ JULY

1 Jul   Unmerc Cosmas & Damian, Rome.
(14/7) *Vn Leontius of Rădăutsi (RO).*

G

2 Jul   Robe of the Theotokos. NC: St
(15/7) John of Shanghai [*or on Sat*].
Oil

F

3 Jul   Mrt Hyacinth. *St Philip, Metr of*
(16/7) *Moscow (relics).*

E

4 Jul   OC, Royal Martyrs (SLV). St
(17/7) Andrew, Archbp of Crete (9th).
OC:oil

D

A person cannot choose the time in which he is born or lives; it is not up to him who his parents are, or the nation he will be born into.
But what he is responsible for, is how he will act in that given time: will he be human or inhuman, no matter his parents or his nation.

+ Patr. Pavle of Serbia

5 Jul	**OC: Vn NwM Elizabeth &**
(18/7)	**Barbara (SLV).** Vn Athanasius,
OC:oil	Ath. *Vn Sergius of Radonezh.*

C

6 Jul	Vn Sisoes the Great. *VgM Lucy.*
(19/7)	*St Juliana of Olshansk (relics).*

B

7 Jul	Vn Thomas of Mt Maleon. *GtM*
(20/7)	*Kyriake [Domnica, Nedelja].*
	SLV: Vn Acacius.

A

✠ JULY

8 Jul   GtM Procopius. *Kazan Icon.*
(21/7) *RO: Mrt Epictetus & Astion.*

G

9 Jul   HrM Pancratius. *Vn Dionysius*
(22/7) *the Orator, of Little St Anne's.*

F

10 Jul Vn Anthony of the Kiev Caves
(23/7) (SLV). 45 Martyrs of Nicopolis.
  Oil   *Placing of the Robe of the Lord.*

E

11 Jul GtM Euphemia. *St Olga (SLV). OC:*
(24/7) *HrM Hilarion of Verey. NC: Repose*
  of Elder Sophrony of Essex.

D

12 Jul Mrt Proclus & Hilarion. *Icon 'Of*
(25/7) *the Three Hands'. NC: Repose*
  of Elder Paisius of Mt Athos.

C

Sunday 13-19 July (26/7-1/8): Celebration of the Holy Fathers of the first Six (or Seven) Oec. Councils [some celebrate esp. the 4th, see p.198].

Is any among you afflicted? Let him pray. Is any merry? Let him sing psalms.

+ *James 5:13*

13 Jul	Synaxis of the Archangel Gabriel.
(26/7)	Vn Stephen the Sabbaite.

B

14 Jul	Ap(70) Aquila. *Vn Nicodemus of*
(27/7)	*the Holy Mountain. St Epiphanius*
	of Cyprus (relics, CY).

A

15 Jul	**EqAp Vladimir of Kiev (SLV).**
(28/7)	Mrt Cyricus & his mother Julitta.
Oil	

G

✢ JULY /August

16 Jul HrM Athenogenes & disciples.
(29/7) *VgM Julia of Carthage. [Some*
also name: 4th Oec. Council]

F

17 Jul **NC: Royal Martyrs (SLV).**
(30/7) GtM Marina [Margaret].
NC:oil

E

18 Jul **NC: Vn NwM Elizabeth &**
(31/7) **Barbara (SLV).** Mrt Emilian.
NC:oil

D

19 Jul **Vn Seraphim of Sarov (relics:**
(1/8) **SLV).** Vn Macrina. Vn Dius.
Oil

C

20 Jul **Prophet Elijah.** *OC: Archpr*
(2/8) *Alexis of Ugine, NwM Nun*
Oil *Maria (Skobtsova) & comp.*

B

Behold, I come quickly:
hold that fast which thou hast,
that no one take thy crown.

+ Rev. 3:11

21 Jul (3/8)	Vn Simeon, Fool-for-Christ & Vn John. *Prophet Ezekiel.* *EL: Mrt Trophimus & comp.*

A

22 Jul (4/8)	EqAp Mary Magdalen. *SLV:* HrM Phocas of Sinope (relics).

G

23 Jul (5/8)	*EL: HrM Phocas of Sinope (relics).* *SLV: Mrt Trophimus & comp.* *Pochaev Icon of the Theotokos.*

F

✤ JULY /August

24 Jul   GtM Christina of Tyre. *Passion-*
(6/8)   *bearers Boris & Gleb (SLV).*

E

25 Jul   Dormition of St Anna. *St*
(7/8)   *Olympias, Deaconess & Vn*
Oil   *Eupraxia. 5th Oec. Council.*

D

26 Jul   HrM Hermolaus & comp. Nun-
(8/8)   Mrt Parasceva [Paraskevi] at Rome.

C

27 Jul   GtM & Physician Panteleimon.
(9/8)   *Sts Clement & comp, disciples of*
Oil   *Sts Cyril & Methodius (BU).*

B

28 Jul   Ap/Dcns Prochorus, Nicanor,
(10/8)   Timon & Parmenas. *Smolensk*
Icon. Vn Irene Chrysovalantou.

A

Procession of the Life-giving Cross: On 1/14 Aug the Cross is brought out during Matins – after the Doxology – and venerated, as on the 3rd Sunday in Lent. (<u>NB: if there is a Vigil, this takes place on the Eve</u>). *Some also:* Lesser Blessing of Water.

Nothing is beyond the power of prayer, except whatever is outside the will of God. *(Greek saying)*

29 Jul   Mrt Callinicus of Gangra. *Mrt*
(11/8)   *Theodota [Theodotia] & sons.*

G

30 Jul   Ap(70) Silas, Silvanus & others.
(12/8)   *HrM Valentine & comp.*
       Vn Angelina of Serbia.

F

31 Jul   **FOREFEAST** of the Cross.
(13/8)   St Eudocimus of Cappadocia.

E

✢ AUGUST

1 Aug   **BEGINNING OF DORMITION FAST.**
(14/8)   **Procession of the Life-giving**
Fast/   **Cross**. Maccabean Martyrs.
SO

D

2 Aug   ProtoM Stephen. *Blessed Basil of*
(15/8)   *Moscow. NC: Archpr Alexis of*
       Ugine, NwM Nun Maria & comp.

C

3 Aug   Vn Isaac, Dalmatus & Faustus. *Vn*
(16/8)   *Anthony the Roman, Novgorod.*

B

4 Aug   The Seven Youths [Sleepers] of
(17/8)   Ephesus. *Mrt Eudocia [Eudoxia].*

A

For details of the **Dormition Fast**, see p.17 (fasting & dispensation) & *HD, p.23, 173* (local custom: *Paraclesis*).

Finally, brethren, whatsoever things are true, whatsoever things are honourable, whatsoever things are just, whatsoever things are pure, whatsoever things are lovely, whatsoever things are of good report; if there be any virtue, and if there be any praise, think on these things.

~ Philippians 4:8

5 Aug	**FOREFEAST**. Martyr Eusignius of
(18/8)	Antioch. *NC: Vn John Jacob of Neamts, the Chozebite (RO).*

G

6 Aug	**+ TRANSFIGURATION +**
(19/8)	*Blessing of the first grapes (and/*
Fish	*or other ripe fruit of the land)*

F

7 Aug	Vn Monk-Mrt Dometius. *St*
(20/8)	*Metrophanes of Voronezh (SLV). Vn Theodora of Sihla (RO).*

E

✤ AUGUST

8 Aug   St Emilian the Confessor.
(21/8)   *Vn Zosimas & Sabbatius of*
          Solovki (relics, SLV).

D

9 Aug   Ap Matthias. *Mrt Anthony of Alx'a.*
(22/8)   *OC: Archpr Alexis of Ugine.*

C

10 Aug   Mrt Archdcn Laurence &comp. *Vn*
(23/8)   *Laurence of Kaluga, Fool-for-XC.*

B

11 Aug   Mrt Archdcn Euplus of Catania.
(24/8)   *Vn Niphon, Patr of C'ple (Ath)*

A

12 Aug   Mrt Anicetus & Photius. *[Tr:*
(25/8)   *Vn Maximus the Confessor].*

G

O ye Apostles, assembled here from the
ends of the earth, bury my body in the
Garden of Gethsemane. And Thou, O my
Son and my God, receive my Spirit.

+ Exaposticarion of
the Dormition

13 Aug (26/8)	**LEAVETAKING**. [Vn Maximus the Confessor. *St Tikhon of Zadonsk*.]

F

14 Aug (27/8)	**FOREFEAST**. Prophet Micah. *Vn Theodosius of the Kiev Caves.*

E

15 Aug **(28/8)** *Fish*	**+ DORMITION OF THE MOST-** **HOLY THEOTOKOS** + *OC: Repose* *Elder Joseph the Hesychast.*

D

�֍ AUGUST /September

16 Aug   **AFTERFEAST. Holy Mandylion.**
(29/8)   Mrt Diomedes. *Prince-Mrt*
   Oil   *Constantine Brâncoveanu (RO).*

C

17 Aug   Mrt Myron of Cyzicus.
(30/8)   *Mrt Straton & comp.*

B

18 Aug   Mrt Florus & Laurus. *Vn Arsenius*
(31/8)   *the New, Paros. OC: Vn John*
       Jacob, the Chozebite.

A

19 Aug   GtM Andrew Stratelates
(1/9)   & 2,593 soldiers with him.

G

20 Aug   Prophet Samuel. *Mrt Reginus*
(2/9)   *& Orestes (CY).*

F

> A sign of humblemindedness is this: that
> when someone possesses every virtue of
> body and soul, he considers himself even
> more in debt to God - because, by His
> grace, he has received so much, whilst
> being unworthy.
>
> *+ Vn Peter of Damascus*

21 Aug **Ap(70) Thaddaeus (c.44)**.
(3/9) *Vn Martha (Maria) of Diveyevo.*
Oil

E

22 Aug Martyr Agathonicus & comp.
(4/9) [*Tr:* Mrt Lupus]. *NC: Archpr
Alexis of Ugine.*

D

23 Aug **LEAVETAKING**. [Mrt Lupus.
(5/9) *HrM Irenaeus, Bp of Lyons*].
Mo:oil

C

✤ AUGUST /September

24 Aug   HrM Eutyches. *EqAp Cosmas*
  (6/9)   *Aitolos. St Peter of Moscow (SLV).*
          OC: NwM priest Maxim Sandovich.

B

25 Aug   Ap(12) Bartholomew (relics).
  (7/9)   Ap(70) Titus, Bp of Gortyna.

A

26 Aug   Icon Vladimirskaya (1395, SLV).
  (8/9)   Mrt Adrian & Natalia. *Vn Joasaph,*
    Oil   *son of King Abenner.*

G

27 Aug   Vn Poemen [Pimen] the Great.
  (9/9)   *GtM Phanurius of Rhodes.*

F

28 Aug   [*Some:* **Leavetk (Mo)**]. Vn Moses
  (10/9)   the Black. *Vn Job of Pochaev. NC:*
            Repose Elder Joseph the Hesychast.

E

Sunday 31 Aug - 6 Sep (13-19/9): Sts Peter & Febronia of Murom (relics, SLV), with special prayers for the family – *see note on p.147.*

Leave the past to God's Mercy,
the present to God's Love,
and the future to His Providence.

+ Abba Hesychius

29 Aug	**BEHEADING OF**
(11/9)	**ST JOHN THE BAPTIST**
Fast/	
SO	

D

30 Aug	**AFTERFEAST** [*one day*]. Sts
(12/9)	Alexander, John & Paul the New,
	of C'ple. *St Alexander Nevsky (SLV).*

C

31 Aug	**Girdle [Sash] of the Theotokos.**
(13/9)	*Vn Eanswyth, Abbess. St Aiden*
Oil	*of Lindisfarne.*

B

SEP/Oct

SPECIAL CELEBRATIONS - SEP/OCT

1 (14/9) Church New Year. Vn Simeon Stylites.
6 (19/9) Miracle Archangel Michael at Colossae/Chonae.
7 (20/9) Forefeast.
8 (21/9) ♦ **Nativity of the Theotokos.**
9 (22/9) Synaxis Sts Joachim & Anna.
11 (24/9) OC: Vn Silouan the Athonite.
12 (25/9) Leavetaking.
13 (26/9) Forefeast of the Cross.
14 (27/9) ♦ **Exaltation (Elevation) of the Life-giving Cross.**
16 (29/9) GtM Euphemia of Chalcedon, the All-Praised.
21 (4/10) Leavetaking.
23 (6/10) Conception of St John the Forerunner.
24 Sep NC: Vn Silouan the Athonite.

OCT/Nov

25 (8/10)   Vn Sergius of Radonezh.
26 (9/10)   ApEv John the Theologian.
28 (11/10) Vn Neophytus the Recluse, Vn Chariton.

SPECIAL CELEBRATIONS - OCT/NOV

1 (14/10)   ♦ **Holy Protection (Pokrov).**
6 (19/10)   Ap Thomas Didymus.
9 (22/10)   Ap James, Son of Alphaeus.
10 (23/10) Vn Ambrose of Optina.
12 (25/10) SLV: Vn Martin the Merciful.
14 (27/10) Vn Parasceva (Petka) of Thrace.
18 (31/10) ApEv Luke.
23 (5/11)   Ap James, Brother of the Lord.
26 (8/11)   GtM Demetrius the Myrrh-flowing.

NOV/Dec

SPECIAL CELEBRATIONS - NOV/DEC

1 (14/11)   Unmercenaries Cosmas & Damian (Asia Minor).
3 (16/11)   GtM George (relics to Lydda).
8 (21/11)   Synaxis Archangels & All the Heavenly Hosts.
9 (22/11)   St Nectarius of Aegina, Bp of Pentapolis.
12 Nov   EL: Vn Martin the Merciful.
13 (26/11) St John Chrysostom.
14 (27/11) Ap(12) Philip. — **15** (28/11) *Beginning Nativity Fast.*
16 (29/11) ApEv Matthew.
20 (3/12)   Forefeast.
21 (4/12)   ♦ **Entry of the Theotokos into the Temple.**
24 (7/12)   SLV: GtM Catherine of Alexandria.
25 (8/12)   Leavetaking. KY/EL: GtM Catherine.
26 (9/12)   Vn Stylianos of Paphlagonia. [KY: Leavetaking].

DEC/Jan

30 (13/12) Ap Andrew, the First-called.

SPECIAL CELEBRATIONS - DEC/JAN

4 (17/12)   GtM Barbara. Vn John of Damascus.
5 (18/12)   Vn Sabbas the Sanctified.
6 (19/12)   St Nicholas of Myra, the Wonderworker.
9 (22/12)   Conception by St Anna.
12 (25/12) St Spyridon. Vn Herman of Alaska.
15 (28/12) HrM Eleutherius.
20 (2/1)   Forefeast. HrM Ignatius. St John of Kronstadt.
24 (6/1)   Eve of the Nativity.
25 (7/1)   ♦ **Nativity in the Flesh of our Lord ICXC.**
26 (8/1)   Synaxis of the Birthgiver of God.
27 (9/1)   Third Day of the Feast. Protomartyr Stephen.
31 (13/1)   Leavetaking of the Nativity.

In the Coming Years

My beloved,
  since you have received
  the blessing of God,
  be prepared to receive trials
  until you have passed beyond them;
then you will have great progress
  and increase in all your virtues,
  and great gladness
  will be given you from heaven,
  such as you have not known.

And the medicine
for passing through the trials
  is that you should not grow weary,
  but pray to God from your whole heart,
  giving thanks and
  showing patience in all things,
then the trial will pass from you.

See how all the saints,
  when they entered into trials,
  called upon God.
Again, it is written,
  "God is faithful;
  He will not suffer you
  to be tried
  beyond your capability".

+ *Abba Ammonas*

AN OVERVIEW OF THE YEAR

- CYCLE OF THE MENAION -

The Eighth Millenium: Besides the year AD (Anno Domini), some also note the years 'from the creation of the world' (AM: Anno Mundi, from 1 Sep): the traditional age of the created world, based on the Septuagint. To find the traditional year, simply add 5508 to the year AD at Pascha – e.g. for Pascha AD 2024 + 5508 = AM 7532 for the liturgical year AD 2023-2024.

✠ SEPTEMBER /Oct

A	1 Sep (14/9)	CHURCH NEW YEAR & Vn Simeon Stylites (o).
G	2 Sep (15/9)	
F	3 Sep (16/9)	
E	4 Sep (17/9)	
D	5 Sep (18/9)	
C	6 Sep (19/9)	Archangel Michael: Miracle at Chonae (o).
B	7 Sep (20/9)	FOREFEAST.
A	**8 Sep (21/9)**	**+ NATIVITY OF THE THEOTOKOS (fs) +**
G	9 Sep (22/9)	Synaxis Rgt Joachim & Anna (o). *3rd Oec. Council.*
F	10 Sep (23/9)	
E	11 Sep (24/9)	OC: Vn Silouan the Athonite (o).
D	12 Sep (25/9)	LEAVETAKING (Mo).
C	13 Sep (26/9)	FOREFEAST. Dedication: Church of the Resurrection (Mo)
B	**14 Sep (27/9)**	**+ EXALTATION OF THE CROSS (fast/SO) +** *6th Oec. Council (EL).*
A	15 Sep (28/9)	

G	16 Sep (29/9)	GtM Euphemia the All-praised (o).
F	17 Sep (30/9)	
E	18 Sep (1/10)	
D	19 Sep (2/10)	
C	20 Sep (3/10)	
B	21 Sep (4/10)	LEAVETAKING.
A	22 Sep (5/10)	
G	23 Sep (6/10)	Conception of St John, Forerunner & Baptist (o).
F	24 Sep (7/10)	NC: Vn Silouan the Athonite (o).
E	25 Sep (8/10)	Vn Sergius of Radonezh (SLV: o).
D	26 Sep (9/10)	ApEv John the Theologian (o).
C	27 Sep (10/10)	
B	28 Sep (11/10)	Vn Neophytus (relics, o).
A	29 Sep (12/10)	
G	30 Sep (13/10)	

✠ OCTOBER /Nov

F	1 Oct (14/10)	POKROV: Holy Protection (o).
E	2 Oct (15/10)	
D	3 Oct (16/10)	
C	4 Oct (17/10)	
B	5 Oct (18/10)	
A	6 Oct (19/10)	Ap(12) Thomas Didymus (o).
G	7 Oct (20/10)	
F	8 Oct (21/10)	
E	9 Oct (22/10)	Ap(12) James of Alphaeus (o).
D	10 Oct (23/10)	Vn Ambrose of Optina (SLV: o) [& *Synaxis Optina Frs*]
C	11 Oct (24/10)	[*Synaxis Optina Frs: today or 10/23 Oct*].
B	12 Oct (25/10)	SLV: St Martin the Merciful (o).
A	13 Oct (26/10)	
G	14 Oct (27/10)	Vn Parasceva (Petka) of Thrace (o).
F	15 Oct (28/10)	

E	16 Oct (29/10)	
D	17 Oct (30/10)	
C	18 Oct (31/10)	ApEv Luke (o).
B	19 Oct (1/11)	
A	20 Oct (2/11)	
G	21 Oct (3/11)	
F	22 Oct (4/11)	
E	23 Oct (5/11)	Ap James, Brother of the Lord (o).
D	24 Oct (6/11)	
C	25 Oct (7/11)	
B	26 Oct (8/11)	GtM Demetrius the Myrrh-flowing (o).
A	27 Oct (9/11)	
G	28 Oct (10/11)	
F	29 Oct (11/11)	
E	30 Oct (12/11)	
D	31 Oct (13/11)	

✠ NOVEMBER /Dec

C	1 Nov (14/11)	Unmerc Cosmas & Damian, from Asia (Mo).
B	2 Nov (15/11)	
A	3 Nov (16/11)	GtM George (relics, o).
G	4 Nov (17/11)	
F	5 Nov (18/11)	
E	6 Nov (19/11)	
D	7 Nov (20/11)	
C	8 Nov (21/11)	Synaxis Archangel Michael & Heavenly Hosts (o).
B	9 Nov (22/11)	St Nectarius of Aegina (o).
A	10 Nov (23/11)	
G	11 Nov (24/11)	
F	12 Nov (25/11)	EL: St John the Merciful & St Martin (o).
E	13 Nov (26/11)	St John Chrysostom (o).
D	14 Nov (27/11)	Ap(12) Philip (o).
C	15 Nov (28/11)	BEGINNING OF THE NATIVITY FAST.

B	16 Nov (29/11)	ApEv Matthew (o).
A	17 Nov (30/11)	
G	18 Nov (1/12)	
F	19 Nov (2/12)	
E	20 Nov (3/12)	FOREFEAST.
D	**21 Nov (4/12)**	**+ THEOTOKOS: ENTRY INTO THE TEMPLE (fs) +**
C	22 Nov (5/12)	
B	23 Nov (6/12)	
A	24 Nov (7/12)	SLV: GtM Catherine of Alexandria (o).
G	25 Nov (8/12)	LEAVETAKING (Mo). EL: GtM Catherine of Alx'ε (o).
F	26 Nov (9/12)	[*KY, transf:* LEAVETAKING *(Mo).*]
E	27 Nov (10/12)	
D	28 Nov (11/12)	
C	29 Nov (12/12)	
B	30 Nov (13/12)	Ap Andrew, the First-called (o).

✤ DECEMBER /Jan

A	1 Dec (14/12)	
G	2 Dec (15/12)	
F	3 Dec (16/12)	
E	4 Dec (17/12)	GtM Barbara. Vn John Damascene (o).
D	5 Dec (18/12)	Vn Sabbas the Sanctified (o).
C	6 Dec (19/12)	St Nicholas of Myra (o).
B	7 Dec (20/12)	
A	8 Dec (21/12)	
G	9 Dec (22/12)	Conception by Rgt Anna (o).
F	10 Dec (23/12)	
E	11 Dec (24/12)	SUN 11/24 - 17/30 DEC: Holy Forefathers.
D	12 Dec (25/12)	St Spyridon (o).
C	13 Dec (26/12)	Vn Herman of Alaska (o),
B	14 Dec (27/12)	
A	15 Dec (28/12)	HrM Eleutherios (o).

G	16 Dec (29/12)	
F	17 Dec (30/12)	Prophet Daniel & the Three Youths (o).
E	18 Dec (31/12)	St Modestus (Mo). SUN BEFORE NATIVITY: 18-24 DEC.
D	19 Dec (1/1)	
C	20 Dec (2/1)	FOREFEAST. HrM Ignatius (o) & Pr John of Kronstadt.
B	21 Dec (3/1)	
A	22 Dec (4/1)	
G	23 Dec (5/1)	
F	24 Dec (6/1)	EVE OF THE NATIVITY (fast/SO).
E	**25 Dec** **(7/1)**	**+ NATIVITY IN THE FLESH OF OUR LORD ICXC +** *(3 days Pascha, FF)*
D	26 Dec (8/1)	Synaxis of the Theotokos. SUN 26-31 DEC: Sts Joseph, David & James.
C	27 Dec (9/1)	Third Day of the Feast.
B	28 Dec (10/1)	
A	29 Dec (11/1)	
G	30 Dec (12/1)	
F	31 Dec (13/1)	LEAVETAKING.

✤ JANUARY /Feb

E	1 Jan (14/1)	CIRCUMCISION ICXC. St Basil the Great.
D	2 Jan (15/1)	FOREFEAST. Vn Seraphim of Sarov.
C	3 Jan (16/1)	
B	4 Jan (17/1)	Synaxis of the Seventy Apostles.
A	5 Jan (18/1)	EVE OF THEOPHANY (fast/SO).
G	**6 Jan (19/1)**	**+ THEOPHANY (FF) +**
F	7 Jan (20/1)	Synaxis of St John the Baptist (fs). SAT/SUN AFTER THEOPHANY (7/20-13/26 Jan).
E	8 Jan (21/1)	
D	9 Jan (22/1)	
C	10 Jan (23/1)	
B	11 Jan (24/1)	Vn Theodosius the Great (o).
A	12 Jan (25/1)	
G	13 Jan (26/1)	
F	14 Jan (27/1)	LEAVETAKING (o).
E	15 Jan (28/1)	

D	16 Jan (29/1)	
C	17 Jan (30/1)	Vn Anthony the Great (o).
B	18 Jan (31/1)	Sts Athanasius & Cyril [Kirill] of Alx'a (o).
A	19 Jan (1/2)	St Mark (Eugenikos) of Ephesus (o).
G	20 Jan (2/2)	Vn Euthymius the Great (o).
F	21 Jan (3/2)	
E	22 Jan (4/2)	OC, SUN 22-28 JAN: Synaxis NwMartyrs & Conf (SLV).
D	23 Jan (5/2)	*6th Oec Council [some on 14/27 Sep].*
C	24 Jan (6/2)	Blessed Xenia of St Petersburg (SLV, o).
B	25 Jan (7/2)	St Gregory the Theologian (o).
A	26 Jan (8/2)	
G	27 Jan (9/2)	St John Chrysostom (relics, o).
F	28 Jan (10/2)	
E	29 Jan (11/2)	
D	30 Jan (12/2)	SYNAXIS OF THE THREE HIERARCHS (o).
C	31 Jan (13/2)	

✚ FEBRUARY /Mar (28)		See next page for leap-years
B	1 Feb (14/2)	FOREFEAST. Martyr Trypon (o). Vn Brigid of Kildare.
A	**2 Feb (15/2)**	**+ MEETING OF THE LORD (fs) +**
G	3 Feb (16/2)	
F	4 Feb (17/2)	NC, SUN 4-10 FEB: Synaxis NwMartyrs & Conf (SLV).
E	5 Feb (18/2)	
D	6 Feb (19/2)	*St Photius [Holy Orth Council: see p.198, HD p.268].*
C	7 Feb (20/2)	
B	8 Feb (21/2)	GtM Theodore Stratelates *[before Lent, Mo:oil].*
A	9 Feb (22/2)	[LEAVETAKING *(before Lent, Mo:oil)*]
G	10 Feb (23/2)	HrM Charalampus [Haralambos] *[before Lent: Oil].*
F	11 Feb (24/2)	
E	12 Feb (25/2)	
D	13 Feb (26/2)	
C	14 Feb (27/2)	
B	15 Feb (28/2)	

A	16 Feb (1/3)	
G	17 Feb (2/3)	GtM Theodore Tyron *[before Lent, Mo:oil]*.
F	18 Feb (3/3)	
E	19 Feb (4/3)	
D	20 Feb (5/3)	
C	21 Feb (6/3)	
B	22 Feb (7/3)	
A	23 Feb (8/3)	
G	24 Feb (9/3)	1st & 2nd Finding of the Head of the Forerunner *[disp, see p.82]*.
F	25 Feb (10/3)	
E	26 Feb (11/3)	
D	27 Feb (12/3)	
C	28 Feb (13/3)	

NB: February 28th is the end of the sequence of weekdays, which starts again on 1 Mar (related to the following Pascha, see Paschal tables). **Paschal Cycle:** The First Sunday of the Triodion can fall between 11 Jan (24/1) – 14 Feb (27/2), depending on the Paschal date.

✛ **FEBRUARY** /Mar (29)	For leap-years, use this table

B	1 Feb (14/2)	FOREFEAST. Martyr Trypon (o). Vn Brigid of Kildare.
A	**2 Feb (15/2)**	**+ MEETING OF THE LORD (fs) +**
G	3 Feb (16/2)	
F	4 Feb (17/2)	NC, SUN 4-10 FEB: Synaxis NwMartyrs & Conf (SLV).
E	5 Feb (18/2)	
D	6 Feb (19/2)	*St Photius [Holy Orth Council: see p.198, HD p.268].*
C	7 Feb (20/2)	
B	8 Feb (21/2)	GtM Theodore Stratelates *[before Lent, Mo:oil].*
A	9 Feb (22/2)	[LEAVETAKING *(before Lent, Mo:oil)*]
G	10 Feb (23/2)	HrM Charalampus [Haralambos] *[before Lent: Oil].*
F	11 Feb (24/2)	
E	12 Feb (25/2)	
D	13 Feb (26/2)	
C	14 Feb (27/2)	
B	15 Feb (28/2)	

	16 Feb	
A	(29/2)	
G	17 Feb (1/3)	GtM Theodore Tyron *[before Lent, Mo:oil]*.
F	18 Feb (2/3)	
E	19 Feb (3/3)	
D	20 Feb (4/3)	
C	21 Feb (5/3)	
B	22 Feb (6/3)	
A	23 Feb (7/3)	
G	24 Feb (8/3)	1st & 2nd Finding of the Head of the Forerunrer *[disp, see p.82]*.
F	25 Feb (9/3)	
E	26 Feb (10/3)	
D	27 Feb (11/3)	
C	28 Feb (12/3)	
B	29 Feb (13/3)	

NB: February 29th is the end of the sequence of weekdays, which starts again on 1 Mar (related to the following Pascha, see Paschal tables).
Paschal Cycle: In leap-years, the First Sunday of the Triodion can fall between 12 Jan (25/1) – 15 Feb (28/2), depending on the Paschal date.

✚ MARCH /Apr

C	1 Mar (14/3)	
B	2 Mar (15/3)	
A	3 Mar (16/3)	
G	4 Mar (17/3)	
F	5 Mar (18/3)	
E	6 Mar (19/3)	
D	7 Mar (20/3)	
C	8 Mar (21/3)	
B	9 Mar (22/3)	Forty Martyrs of Sebaste *[disp, see p.82]*.
A	10 Mar (23/3)	
G	11 Mar (24/3)	
F	12 Mar (25/3)	
E	13 Mar (26/3)	
D	14 Mar (27/3)	
C	15 Mar (28/3)	

B	16 Mar (29/3)	
A	17 Mar (30/3)	
G	18 Mar (31/3)	
F	19 Mar (1/4)	
E	20 Mar (2/4)	
D	21 Mar (3/4)	
C	22 Mar (4/4)	
B	23 Mar (5/4)	
A	24 Mar (6/4)	FOREFEAST.
G	**25 Mar** **(7/4)**	**+ ANNUNCIATION +** *[disp, see p.82]*
F	26 Mar (8/4)	*[Synaxis Archangel Gabriel.]*
E	27 Mar (9/4)	
D	28 Mar (10/4)	
C	29 Mar (11/4)	
B	30 Mar (12/4)	
A	31 Mar (13/4)	

✦ APRIL /May

G	1 Apr (14/4)
F	2 Apr (15/4)
E	3 Apr (16/4)
D	4 Apr (17/4)
C	5 Apr (18/4)
B	6 Apr (19/4)
A	7 Apr (20/4)
G	8 Apr (21/4)
F	9 Apr (22/4)
E	10 Apr (23/4)
D	11 Apr (24/4)
C	12 Apr (25/4)
B	13 Apr (26/4)
A	14 Apr (27/4)
G	15 Apr (28/4)

F	16 Apr (29/4)	
E	17 Apr (30/4)	
D	18 Apr (1/5)	
C	19 Apr (2/5)	
B	20 Apr (3/5)	
A	21 Apr (4/5)	
G	22 Apr (5/5)	
F	23 Apr (6/5)	GtM George (*after Lent*, o).
E	24 Apr (7/5)	
D	25 Apr (8/5)	ApEv Mark (*after Lent*, o).
C	26 Apr (9/5)	
B	27 Apr (10/5)	
A	28 Apr (11/5)	
G	29 Apr (12/5)	
F	30 Apr (13/5)	Ap James of Zebedee, brother of St John (o).

✤ MAY /June

E	1 May (14/5)	
D	2 May (15/5)	St Athanasius (relics, Mo).
C	3 May (16/5)	Vn Theodosius of the Kiev Caves (SLV, o).
B	4 May (17/5)	
A	5 May (18/5)	
G	6 May (19/5)	
F	7 May (20/5)	
E	8 May (21/5)	ApEv John the Theologian (o).
D	9 May (22/5)	
C	10 May (23/5)	
B	11 May (24/5)	EqAp Methodius & Cyril (SLV, o).
A	12 May (25/5)	
G	13 May (26/5)	
F	14 May (27/5)	
E	15 May (28/5)	St Pachomius the Great (o).

D	16 May (29/5)	
C	17 May (30/5)	
B	18 May (31/5)	
A	19 May (1/6)	
G	20 May (2/6)	
F	21 May (3/6)	EqAp Constantine & Helena (o).
E	22 May (4/6)	*2nd Oec. Council.*
D	23 May (5/6)	
C	24 May (6/6)	
B	25 May (7/6)	3rd Finding of the Head of the Forerunner (Mc).
A	26 May (8/6)	
G	27 May (9/6)	
F	28 May (10/6)	
E	29 May (11/6)	OC: St Luke of Simferopol (SLV, o). *[1st Oec. Council]* .
D	30 May (12/6)	
C	31 May (13/6)	

✦ JUNE / July

B	1 Jun (14/6)	
A	2 Jun (15/6)	
G	3 Jun (16/6)	
F	4 Jun (17/6)	
E	5 Jun (18/6)	
D	6 Jun (19/6)	
C	7 Jun (20/6)	
B	8 Jun (21/6)	
A	9 Jun (22/6)	
G	10 Jun (23/6)	
F	11 Jun (24/6)	Ap Barnabas & Barth. (o). NC: St Luke of Simferopol.
E	12 Jun (25/6)	
D	13 Jun (26/6)	
C	14 Jun (27/6)	
B	15 Jun (28/6)	

A	16 Jun (29/6)	
G	17 Jun (30/6)	
F	18 Jun (1/7)	
E	19 Jun (2/7)	Ap Jude, brother XC (o). OC: St John of Shanghai [*or Sat*]
D	20 Jun (3/7)	
C	21 Jun (4/7)	
B	22 Jun (5/7)	
A	23 Jun (6/7)	
G	**24 Jun (7/7)**	**NATIVITY OF ST JOHN, Forerunner & Baptist** (fs).
F	25 Jun (8/7)	AFTERFEAST [*one day*].
E	26 Jun (9/7)	
D	27 Jun (10/7)	
C	28 Jun (11/7)	
B	**29 Jun (12/7)**	**AP. PETER & PAUL** (fs).
A	30 Jun (13/7)	Synaxis of the Twelve Apostles (o).

✠ JULY /Aug

G	1 Jul (14/7)	
F	2 Jul (15/7)	Robe of Theotokos (o). NC: St John of Shanghai [*or Sat*]
E	3 Jul (16/7)	
D	4 Jul (17/7)	OC: Royal Martyrs (SLV, o).
C	5 Jul (18/7)	OC: NwM Elizabeth & Barbara (SLV, o).
B	6 Jul (19/7)	
A	7 Jul (20/7)	
G	8 Jul (21/7)	
F	9 Jul (22/7)	
E	10 Jul (23/7)	Vn Anthony, Kiev Caves (SLV, o).
D	11 Jul (24/7)	*GtM Euphemia: Miracle at 4th Oec. Council, Chalcedon.*
C	12 Jul (25/7)	
B	13 Jul (26/7)	
A	14 Jul (27/7)	
G	15 Jul (28/7)	EqAp Vladimir of Kiev (SLV, o).

F	16 Jul (29/7)	[*4th Oec. Council*]
E	17 Jul (30/7)	NC: Royal Martyrs (SLV, o).
D	18 Jul (31/7)	NC: Vn NwM Elizabeth & Barbara (SLV, o).
C	19 Jul (1/8)	Vn Seraphim of Sarov, relics (SLV, o).
B	20 Jul (2/8)	Prophet Elijah [Elias] (o).
A	21 Jul (3/8)	
G	22 Jul (4/8)	
F	23 Jul (5/8)	
E	24 Jul (6/8)	
D	25 Jul (7/8)	Dormition of St Anna (o). *5th Oec. Council.*
C	26 Jul (8/8)	
B	27 Jul (9/8)	GtM Panteleimon (o).
A	28 Jul (10/8)	
G	29 Jul (11/8)	
F	30 Jul (12/8)	
E	31 Jul (13/8)	FOREFEAST.

✦ AVGVST /Sep

D	1 Aug (14/8)	BEGINNING DORMITION FAST. Procession of the Cross.
C	2 Aug (15/8)	
B	3 Aug (16/8)	
A	4 Aug (17/8)	
G	5 Aug (18/8)	FOREFEAST.
F	**6 Aug** **(19/8)**	**+ TRANSFIGURATION (fs) +**
E	7 Aug (20/8)	
D	8 Aug (21/8)	
C	9 Aug (22/8)	
B	10 Aug (23/8)	
A	11 Aug (24/8)	
G	12 Aug (25/8)	
F	13 Aug (26/8)	LEAVETAKING.
E	14 Aug (27/8)	FOREFEAST.
D	**15 Aug** **(28/8)**	**+ DORMITION OF THE THEOTOKOS (fs) +**

	16 Aug (29/8)	AFTERFEAST. Holy Mandylion (o).
C		
B	17 Aug (30/8)	
A	18 Aug (31/8)	
G	19 Aug (1/9)	
F	20 Aug (2/9)	
E	21 Aug (3/9)	Ap(70) Thaddaeus (o).
D	22 Aug (4/9)	
C	23 Aug (5/9)	LEAVETAKING (Mo).
B	24 Aug (6/9)	
A	25 Aug (7/9)	
G	26 Aug (8/9)	Vladimirskaya (1395, SLV, o).
F	27 Aug (9/9)	
E	28 Aug (10/9)	[*postponed: Leavetaking (Mo)*]
D	**29 Aug** **(11/9)**	**BEHEADING OF ST JOHN THE BAPTIST (fast/SO).**
C	30 Aug (12/9)	AFTERFEAST [*one day*].
B	31 Aug (13/9)	Girdle [Sash] of the Theotokos (o).

In Short (*for further details see HD, p.264-ff*)

HOLY ORTHODOX COVNCILS

♦ **1: Nicaea, AD 325** *(318 Frs) – Sun. before Pentecost, some also on 29 May (11/6).* Jesus Christ is truly both God and man (*homo-ousios:* consubstantial, one in essence). First formulation of the Creed. [*Also:* standard for the Paschal celebration].

♦ **2: Constantinople, AD 381** *(150 Frs) – 22 May (4/6).* The Holy Spirit is truly God, originating from the Father. The Holy Trinity exists as a unity of three divine *Hypostases* – who are one in *essence* (*ousia*), but distinct as to the uniqueness of each *hypostasis/person.* Final formulation of the Creed (Nicaea-C'ple).

♦ **3: Ephesus, AD 431/33** *(200 Frs) – 9 Sep (22/9).* Confirmation of the ancient title *Theotokos:* The person of Jesus Christ is truly God Incarnate.

♦ **4: Chalcedon, AD 451** *(630 Frs) – 11 July (24/7) [some also on 16/29 July, and/or Sun 13-19 July].* (Refuting monophysitism) In Christ, the two *natures* – divine/uncreated & human/created – are united in one single *Person (Hypostasis),* without division and without confusion. [*Also:* Pentarchy & Cyprus].

♦ **5: C'ple, AD 553** *(165 Frs) – 25 July (7/8).* Confirmation & further clarification concerning the two natures united in the one person of Christ.

♦ **6: C'ple, AD 680/81** *(170 Frs) – commemorated 23 Jan (5/2), EL: 14 Sep (27/9).* (Refuting monotheletism) The insight concerning the two natures in one person includes *all* aspects of each nature (except sin). *Salvation basically means to be united with God, 'in Christ'* – and *'that which is not assumed* [in the person of Jesus Christ] *is not healed' (St Gregory the Theologian).*

♦ **7: Nicaea, AD 787** *(350 Frs) – Sunday ca. 11/24 Oct.* Concerning the use and veneration of the Holy Icons.

♦ **The Triumph of Orthodoxy: AD 842** – *celebrated on the First Sunday of Lent.*

♦ **The first Six (or Seven) Oecumenical Councils**
  – *commemorated together on Sunday 13-19 July.*

The following Orthodox Councils are equally crucial for a proper understanding of the ancient Christian Faith:

♦ **8: C'ple, AD 879** *(383 Frs)* – *6 Feb (St Photius).* Accepting & confirming St Photius' refutation of the *filioque* (this addition to the Creed denies the unity and equality of the holy Trinity).

♦ **9: C'ple, AD 1341 & 1351** – *upholding the teaching of St Gregory Palamas, celebrated 2nd Sunday of Lent.* Clarifying the distinction between the Divine *Essence* and *Energies.* True union with God is indeed possible, when man is filled with the *uncreated grace* (energy) of God.

I am the Way, the Truth, and the Life.
(Jn.14:6)

RANKS OF THE HOLY ANGELS

The Angelic Powers are arranged in nine ranks, according to their functions (NB: some translations vary):

The fiery six-winged Seraphim, the many-eyed Cherubim, and godly Thrones; Dominions (Κυριότητες), Authorities (Ἐξουσίες), and Principalities (Ἄρχοντες); Powers (Δύναμεις), Archangels and Angels.

The Archangels, leaders of the Heavenly Hosts (8/21 Nov):

♦ ***Michael*** – *'who is like God?'* or *'who is equal to God?'* (leader of the Heavenly Hosts; guardian/protector of the true Faith).

♦ ***Gabriel*** – *'Man of God',* or *'Power of God'/'God is Mighty'* (herald of the mysteries of God, esp. the Incarnation).

♦ ***Raphael*** – *'God's healing',* or *'God is Healer'* (with Tobias).

♦ ***Uriel*** – *'fire'* or *'light of God'* (II Esdras 4:1, 5:20).

♦ ***Salathiel*** – *'one who prays to God'* (II Esdras 5:16).

♦ ***Jegudiel*** – *'one who glorifies God'.*

♦ ***Barachiel*** – *'the blessing of God'.*

♦ ***Jeremiel*** – *'God's exaltation'* (higher thoughts, God-ward).

These things I have spoken unto you,
that in Me ye might have peace.
In the world ye shall have tribulation:
but be of good cheer;
I have overcome the world.

+ *John 16:33*

ΑΩ

The End and Glory Be to God

And I saw a new heaven and a new earth: for the first heaven and the first earth were passed away; and there was no more sea. And I John saw the holy city, new Jerusalem, coming down from God out of heaven, prepared as a bride adorned for her husband. And I heard a great voice out of heaven saying, Behold, the tabernacle of God is with men, and he will dwell with them, and they shall be his people, and God himself shall be with them, and be their God. And God shall wipe away all tears from their eyes; and there shall be no more death, neither sorrow, nor crying, neither shall there be any more pain: for the former things are passed away. And he that sat upon the throne said, Behold, I make all things new.

+ Revelation 21:1-5 (kjv)

www.ingramcontent.com/pod-product-compliance
Lightning Source LLC
Chambersburg PA
CBHW051435090426
42737CB00014B/2982

* 9 781917 556019 *